This inspiring b[illegible] the hand and walks you through every step you need to find healing from all sorts of trauma that life can bring. Carol's transparency, vulnerability, and humour will open your heart as she leads you on the journey from *There to Here*. Read it, engage the disciplines, and allow God to transform you in the deepest levels of your being, and experience life to the fullest.

—Lori Crawford, Senior Leadership
Centralia Faith Tabernacle Equipping Centre

Beginning with the first page, it is very obvious that Carol has the ability to tell a spectacular story. One of the most amazing things about it is that it is all true. You will walk with her through the valleys and climb to the mountaintops of her journey of tears, faith, and triumph.

—George Woodward
St. Catharines, Ontario

Although I have never been personally through the trials and trauma of a car accident, I have been through this journey with many patients. I always thought I understood the complexity of the trauma and struggle to recovery for my patients, but this book has made me realize it is so much more. I can't possibly understand the depth of a patients suffering in a fifteen-minute appointment.

From the physician perspective, traumatic brain injuries can be frustrating. Since the healing course often waxes and wanes, we go through a lot of treatment failure, and patients continue to suffer, leading the physician to feel defeated. Your book has definitely served as a reminder of hope for both patients and health care practitioners.

I think in situations when hope is lost, having faith and spirituality are extremely important, and are often overlooked by doctors today. This book is an excellent reminder and serves as anecdotal evidence for the role of spirituality in healing. So much time and energy is spent with doctors, chiropractors, massage therapists, physical therapists, dentists, psychologists, and so on, just as Carol describes in her book. These are all taught to young medical practitioners as therapeutic options for brain trauma. What is lacking is the spiritual aspect. More time should be considered for faith and spirituality. In the future, I will be able to recommend this to the right patients in my practice.

An inspiring read for anyone who has suffered, or is currently suffering from, any level of trauma.

—Dr. Andrew Prout, MD, CCFP, MSc

Carol has written a must-read for anyone on a journey of recovery and restoration from one of life's many unexpected traumas. From her own personal experience, Carol shares from an authentic genuine heart with unashamed transparency and hope, sprinkled with her inspiring humour; she is determined to see others move *From There to Here*.

—Cathy Prout, Senior Pastor
Centralia Faith Tabernacle Equipping Centre

Carol takes the reader through her desperate journey to find relief from her chronic pain after her car accident. In her search, she finds not just physical relief, but discovers a closer relationship with God that had been guiding her every step. A must read for all those living with chronic pain.

—Dr. Mary Elliott Huyzen, PhD

FINDING VICTORY FROM THERE TO HERE AFTER TRAUMA

BY CAROL CYR

FROM THERE TO HERE

Printed in Canada

ISBN: 978-1-4866-1575-9

Word Alive Press
119 De Baets Street, Winnipeg, MB R2J 3R9
www.wordalivepress.ca

WORD ALIVE
—PRESS—

FSC
www.fsc.org
MIX
Paper from responsible sources
FSC® C016245

Cataloguing in Publication may be obtained through Library and Archives Canada

This book is dedicated to my husband, Dave.

His calm and steadfast manner has held me steady when the waves were above my head.

Thank you for being you!

TABLE OF CONTENTS

SHOUT OUTS

Thank you, Jesus, for pulling me up from under and placing me in heavenly places right next to you.

Thank you to my husband, Dave, who has stood with me and supported me without complaint or doubt that I would push through into victory. His constant love through difficult days continues to be an anchor for me. His patience is never ending.

To my children, Adam and his wife Crystal, and Nikki and Casey, and to my G-children to date, Warren, Quinn, and Lucy: You allowed me to be me and showed me that it doesn't matter what I can or cannot do, I am still loved and valuable and can contribute in ways I never thought possible.

To my mentor, pastor, and friend, Cathy Prout: I appreciate your sacrifice in helping me see the real me. Thank you for being the shepherd God has made you. You are not afraid to come after the one sheep. I can't imagine what life would be like without you as a friend. You make me laugh.

To my friend and teacher, Lori Crawford: You are such an encourager, and I am blessed beyond what you will ever know to have you in my life. Without your support and encouragement, this book would not be what it is, and the potential for others that lies within these pages would not have come to reality.

To my editors, Lori Crawford, Casey Cyr, Nikki Cyr, Maggie Jinks, and Yvonne Reynolds: Thank you for dotting the i's and crossing the t's in the right places.

To the team at Word Alive Press: Thank you for all of your encouragement and help.

Nikki Cyr, thank you for helping me to publish this book. The cover is the best, and you never cease to amaze me with the way you are using the gifts God has given you.

To my many friends and relatives and all those who had their part to play: You played it well; thank you.

May God multiply back into all your lives all you have poured into me.

Blessings to all.

—Carol Cyr

FOREWORD

What do you do when you encounter an out-of-your-control experience that takes your life in the "here" and hides it over "there"? You begin a brave and courageous journey of restoration!

Carol's journey of recovery and restoration is a powerful and timely message of hope. Many of us hold great aspirations for our lives, but we're often hindered by events and circumstances. We're not meant to live under our experiences or be trapped by them. Carol's message has the transformational power to liberate anyone stuck in a cycle of hopelessness and despair.

I am inspired and encouraged as I read this book, because there is life and hope found in its pages. It's a comprehensive and holistic guide to progressing through trauma and pain of all sorts—emotional, physical, and spiritual. I'm confident that by reading and implementing the truths found in this book, people will regain what they have lost.

Carol's personal stories and declarations will infuse the reader with hope to believe for and apprehend recovery from pain and/or loss. Her writing provides a brilliant context for the struggles we face in our emotional and physical world, while creating a solid pathway to step into new realms of health and wholeness.

Carol is a woman of deep faith, courage, and perseverance. She has authority in the area of restoration because she has journeyed through it, discovering how to partner with truth to change the way she thinks. Each chapter contains strategic keys to empowering one to live on top of the out-of-control experience that introduced a path of pain. I believe these keys will unlock greater freedom and healing in each life.

I am so proud of Carol as her pastor, mentor, and friend. She is real, raw, and relational— not to mention, hilariously funny. She took something that was designed to bring her destiny to a halt and repurposed it to catapult her into that destiny, helping countless others to do the same. I watched as she wrestled and won. I watched as she wanted to quit but didn't. I watched her determine that the abundant life promised to her was going to be hers, and indeed it is! Most of all, I watched her steadfastly journey from there to here.

—Pastor Cathy Prout

Centralia Faith Tabernacle Equipping Centre

Are you tired?
Are you worn out?
Are you burned out on doing things your way?
Come to me. Get away with me and you'll recover your life.
Walk with me and work with me; watch how I do it.
Learn the unforced rhythms of grace.
I won't lay anything heavy or ill-fitting on you.
Keep company with me, and you will learn to live freely and lightly.

Author
Jesus of Nazareth
Son of God
Matthew 11:28 30 (paraphrased)
The Message

THE BEGINNING

Trauma changes everything. It's that split second that our whole world comes crashing down, or the slow and repetitive assault of needs not being met that wears on us day after day. It's the feeling of a deep, deep loss that lodges itself in the core of our being; it's hopelessness at its finest hour.

When an unexpected trauma in 2008 launched me onto a path that threatened to take me out, I had some choices to make. I was left stranded somewhere between wanting to die and wanting to fight. No matter which path I decided to take, I was going to have to face pain that I, myself, would have never chosen to look at.

While it's important to understand that God is never the source of trauma, He can and will use everything that happens in our lives to cause us to come into the fullness of who He created us to be. There is no situation too dark for God to come and set us free from. He brings strategies, healing, and wholeness in ways that are unique to each person and each situation.

As you read through my story, you'll hear of the ways God not only moved me through trauma, but used it to reveal dark areas and transform me into the woman He had always called me to be. Only God can do that.

No matter what trauma you have faced, whether it was caused by a sudden loss or a slow leak of life over the years, God has a way through the pain. There is another side. My prayer is that you would take each part of my story as an opportunity to open your heart and hear what God is saying to you. I've included some tools that helped me move through the reality of the pain and fear of what my future would look like after trauma.

I believe that you have picked up this book for this moment. Allow God to help you let go of where you used to be in order to embrace who He's created you to be. The journey ahead isn't an easy road, but there is a fullness awaiting you on the other side and a God who loves you and wants to walk with you through every twist and turn. The most important thing you could ever know as you continue to move ahead on your journey is this—you are not alone.

CHAPTER ONE

THE TRAUMA

I didn't hear the sirens. Maybe they all came in silence—the police, ambulance, and fire trucks—each one hoping for the best but expecting that it could be the worst. I remember driving down the highway, cruising along on Thursday, March 13, 2008. Groceries had been purchased, Ruth Fazal was playing *Songs of the River*, and Friday was coming. Life was grand. For the first time in my life, I felt like I was living the dream.

I saw the truck stopped on the right side of the intersection ahead and a car coming from the left side. I had the right of way at this intersection, but the car to my left looked like it wasn't going to stop. All at once it was a blur of thoughts: *That car isn't slowing down! What do I do? Where can I go? God help me!* There was nowhere to go but straight ahead, so I held on tight, slammed the brakes hard, and right before my eyes saw the side mirror of a silver vehicle. In the midst of such chaos, I had never felt such peace and tranquility as I did in those few seconds before my life changed forever.

I remember gasping as I woke up, and I saw everything through a white veil. I instantly thought, *I'm in Heaven*. I was so happy, rejoicing inside. Then reality hit like a sledgehammer. It felt as if someone had stuck a knife in my neck, and it was still there. That's when I knew I wasn't in Heaven. I heard

Ruth playing on as if nothing had happened. I looked around and saw that the rear-view mirror was missing, and then I thought my car was on fire, because everything looked whitish through the veil. I knew it wasn't air bag dust, because I had contact lenses in my eyes and they didn't hurt (this will be an important fact later on in my story). When I looked out the window, I thought I was in a foreign land. Nothing looked familiar to me, yet I still had this peace and calm that can only be explained as the presence of God.

A young man walked up to my car to talk to me. All I wanted to do was get out of my burning car. The peace allowed me to hear and believe him when he assured me my car wasn't on fire. My only disappointment was when he turned off the key—Ruth went silent.

Time moved slowly for me during that half hour. Friends who were nearby came quickly to help. She, an ex-paramedic, held my head still and spoke encouraging words to me. I hope she has since received the loving kindness she showed me that day. Her husband, a volunteer firefighter, was there as well, doing what firefighters do. They certainly were in the right place at the right time for me. God provides what we need when we need it, and I have seen throughout this journey that God was everywhere ... I just had to open my eyes.

It's really quite amazing to me that they moved a five-foot-eight-inch woman with long legs out of a scrunched-up Toyota Echo without me moving my body. My job was to stay still. It's a hard task when you're very uncomfortable. It's a little odd to think about now, but from the time I was taken from my squished vehicle until I was allowed to sit up, all I saw was up—the open sky, the roof of an ambulance, the ceiling of hospital corridors, and people looking down at me. A whole different perspective! That was just the beginning of the change in my outlook.

Lying on a stretcher in the back of an ambulance isn't as exciting as some may think. I was very upset when they cut my clothes off, because I had on a brand-new vest and my favourite pants. (A side note here: It was good advice when your mother encouraged you to wear clean underwear when you go out because you just never know what may unfold in a day.)

Stripped of my clothing, it was now time to answer a ton of questions. The paramedics couldn't seem to remember the day, my name, or what happened, because they kept asking me. I know now it was to see if I had a serious head injury, but at the time it seemed like a lot to ask when all I wanted to do was shut my eyes and rest. Didn't they know I was just in a car accident? That takes a lot out of a person! It's really quite funny what goes through a person's mind when they get thrown around a bit.

I was taken to the hospital to be put to the test. A quick wave to my family—they made it to the hospital before I did—then onward to be examined. A person needs prayer before being examined by any ER doctor, because it hurts. They didn't give me drugs until after the examination—and if I didn't need them before, I certainly needed them after. Next I went to the X-ray department, with more gazing at the ceiling as we rolled down the hall. This part still brings a slight stirring in my stomach when I recall how they pushed me up to a sitting position. It felt like my stomach was going to come out the top of my head and take my brains with it as it spilled onto my lap. The good news is that I did survive. After all the testing was done, my family helped me hobble to the car, dressed in donated clothes from my son. The dream life I had just started living began to take a new turn.

THE GOD FACTOR

> Trauma: a very difficult or unpleasant experience that causes someone. To have mental or emotional problems, usually for a long time.

Life sometimes takes unexpected twists and turns that we have no control over. We aren't given the choice, like when we're faced with a crossroad. Trauma happens and we are never the same afterwards. We have the choice to move forward or remain where we are, because we cannot go back, even though we certainly try to.

I am a born again, spirit-filled believer in Jesus Christ, the Son of God, and all that goes with Him and His Kingdom. I am convinced of this, because I met God up-close and personal and have had encounter after encounter with Him. You cannot convince me otherwise. On June 5, 2005, I met Jesus for the first time. Although I'd known about him for forty-six years of my life, I'd never really met him. Once you meet face to face with Love, you won't be the same. Most of us have no idea of the true meaning of love, but I've had a taste of love, and it's worth everything to me. I'll spend the rest of my life chasing after Love, Jesus Christ.

The day of my car accident changed my life dramatically. Like everyone else, I asked the question, "Why, God?" I certainly don't have all the answers, and even though He has shared with me some reasons, I won't write about it now. I will say, though, that God wants to take the worst that can happen and use it for our best. God is good; there is no evil in Him, but there is an evil in this world, and his name is satan. God created us to have free will, and we must choose to follow God's path for us if we want to see His best. I was determined that I wouldn't be one of the ones who gave up and settled for "good." I wanted the best, because God said I was worth the best He has for me. The only way to know God's path is to have a relationship with His Son, because He is the only way to Father God.

To deny there is a God is just not logical. To deny that He is good is also not logical. I have read the instruction manual and learned about the God who made the universe, the galaxies, the sun, the sky, the earth, and most importantly, me in His image. I've asked Him to let me see things His way, from His perspective, and what a ride it continues to be. My point is that you must at least try wholeheartedly to have a relationship with the God who made you, who knew you before you were formed in your mother's womb. The key word is *wholeheartedly*. God designed each of us with a spot that only He can fill. Jesus fills that desire we have for wholeness. When you experience trauma, Jesus is the way to the restoration of who God made you to be. You will not be disappointed when you surrender your all to Jesus.

To help you practically apply what you've read, I've placed at the end of each chapter questions to consider, scriptures to decree out loud, and a personal prayer. I will also include further reading for you to explore greater depths of the God who made you and loves you.

GOING DEEPER

REFLECTION

1. Have you been involved in some form of trauma? It doesn't have to be on a large scale to have had a serious impact on your emotional or mental well-being. Write down the incident and any mental, physical, or emotional side-effects you can identify.

2. Do you have a relationship with Jesus?
   a) If so, you are connected to the One who will connect you to your wholeness. He will help you walk through this healing process.
   b) If not, consider beginning a relationship with Him. He wants to lead you and guide you down the path to restoration and wholeness.

DECREE

This is how much God loved the world: He gave his Son, his one and only Son. And this is why: so that no one need be destroyed; by believing in him, anyone can have a whole and lasting life. God didn't go to all the trouble of sending his Son merely to point an accusing finger, telling the world how bad it was. He came to help, to put the world right again. Anyone who trusts in him is acquitted; anyone who refuses to trust him has long since been under the death sentence without knowing it. And why? Because of that person's failure to believe in the one-of-a-kind Son of God when introduced to Him. (John 3:16–18, MSG) If you openly declare that Jesus is Lord and believe in your heart that God raised him from the dead, you will be saved (Romans 10:9).

PRAYER

God, I know You are real. I want to learn about You. I want to learn about who I am. I believe Jesus died for my sins on a cross. I believe He died and rose from the dead and is now in Heaven, interceding for me. I ask that you would forgive me for my sins, and I invite the Spirit of Jesus, Holy Spirit, to come into my heart and heal me and teach me how to live in the Kingdom of God. I give my life to You, Jesus, and decree You are Lord of my life. My life that You gave to me as a gift I now give back to You. Teach me Your ways, teach me the truth, and teach me how to really live life. Amen.

FURTHER READING

1 John 4 (You can download the Bible App which has many versions of the Word of God right at your fingertips.)

The Cross by Cathy Ciaramitaro, Milestones International Publishers, 2006

CHAPTER TWO

FALLING DOWN

I came home from the hospital to my couch. I thought I could finally get some sleep, but the doctor ordered me to be awakened every few hours. Later I would find out that this girl wouldn't have a decent sleep for three more years.

The first couple of weeks are a little fuzzy for me. I do remember the visits from friends, checking in as if there was something seriously wrong with me. I can't forget the bruises all over my body and the excruciating pain in my right knee. I couldn't get up by myself that first week, struggling to even get to the bathroom. I needed help to stay standing up until I felt like I was balanced.

A couple of days after my accident I remember lying on my new bed—the couch—and hearing a loud bang. Dave, my husband, was doing something in the basement, and I thought in my fuzzy mind that he must have fallen down the stairs. The noise was kind of eerie and drawn-out. I yelled a few times, maybe more than a few, and was just getting ready to roll off the couch and crawl to the basement door when he came around the corner. I don't know if I was happier that he wasn't hurt or that I didn't have to crawl on the floor to find him. He looked around and discovered the under part of our roof had fallen to the ground. It turned out that not just a part had fallen, but almost three quarters of the soffit lay in an unusual border around our house. Not a pretty sight in the middle of March. A lot of things were falling apart at that time. I know now it was the beginning of the unravelling of my entire life. It was the start of the letting go process that I had no idea was even happening. Who really knows the end result of the process when it begins?

I went to see my family doctor the following week and was given drugs for pain and sleeping, as well as directions to take physiotherapy. Somewhere in between going to see my doctor and going to physiotherapy, I purchased a new car. I don't recall much about that purchase, but I bought a new Toyota Yaris in the colour blue. Something seems very wrong with this as I think about it today, because I'm not a big fan of blue. I like black. Nonetheless, I came home with a signed paper that said I was the owner of a brand new blue car.

The first time I drove after the accident I was experiencing the start of a head cold with watery eyes and a runny nose. It was near the end of March, a typical winter day—very snowy, blowy, and the roads looked slippery. To give you some background, I live in the snowbelt area of Southwestern Ontario. It wasn't a great day to get back in the driver's seat, but I wouldn't be intimidated. I started off to the doctor's office to get a drug refill, then on to my first physiotherapy appointment.

I don't know what I was thinking, but I wasn't prepared for the pain that physiotherapy was going to cause. Regardless, I dove right in, working very hard to the point of throwing up to "make" myself better. I had a wrong attitude and a wrong mindset. I thought that the harder I worked, the harder I put myself into the task at hand, the quicker this would be over and the sooner I would be back to normal. Boy, was I wrong.

Because of the wrong thinking embedded deep inside of me, I was, in fact, on the way to a deep, dark place that would eventually try to overtake me.

THE UNRAVELLING

Unravel:

1. a) to disengage or separate the threads of;
   b) to cause to come apart by or as if by separating the threads of.
2. to resolve the intricacy, complexity or obscurity of: clear up (unravel a mystery).

Before we can deal with our trauma issues, we must come to the realization that we have a problem. God wants the best for us, and often that looks very different than what we thought. I thought I'd be back to my normal self in no time. I'd do what I was told to do and work really hard, and everything would return to the way it was before the accident. I didn't have the revelation that God is constantly moving forward, so there was no way for me to go back. God had given me a sign: the rotting old building of my life was coming down, just as my roof had.

I didn't know that at the time. I've since learned how to see the signs He leaves for me. God speaks to us every day, but most of us aren't listening or looking. We feel all alone, even when God is right there ... as close as our next breath. Ask Him to open your eyes so you can see. Holy Spirit (the third person of God) is here on earth to help us when circumstances overwhelm us and we don't know how to resolve or deal with them. We don't have to do life alone. I regret that it took me so long to realize that help is available for me every day, all day long, and I only need to ask. It's a humbling thing to do, but the Bible says, "*When you call on me, when you come and pray to me, I'll listen. When you come looking for me, you'll find me*" (Jeremiah 29:12–13a, MSG). Wait a minute! This is a promise of God that's activated by me asking and seeking Him! How simple is that?

If you resist God's way of doing things, He will let you go your own way until you come to the end of yourself. The unravelling and untwisting of Carol came at great cost to my pride. Although we're at the beginning of my story, I am already "from there to here," so I'm writing from a different perspective. A process cannot really begin until you submit yourself to God. When you do that, you're saying, "I don't know what to do here; help me get through this."

Pride will twist how and what you hear people say. For the most part, pride wants you to do things on your own, when what you really need is help to learn and grow in the ways of the Kingdom of God. It's true that it takes a village to raise a child, especially a Kingdom child. Pride or any other sin you are dealing with is not really who you are or who God made you to be. It's something that has invaded your space and is trying to take over your thoughts through strongholds and wrong patterns of thinking that have been developed over years. Pride will keep you isolated, because you really don't trust that anyone knows more than you.

Looking back, I know now that when our roof fell down, it was a sign from God. The old coverings, the old patterns of life, were going to come down, and a new covering was going to be established. Things were going to change. They had to change for me to move forward at the speed God wanted to move me. The enemy had tried to kill me—that was reality.

God was going to take what the enemy did and raise me up, clean me up, and set me in heavenly places that I could only dream about. He was going to train me in Kingdom ways that in reality should have taken me many years to achieve. I was on an accelerated path. Looking back, I can say that it was the most amazing adventure I'd been on in my whole life ... so far, that is. It's even more amazing that this isn't just for me. God wants to take you on your own amazing journey of discovering yourself and unravelling the mystery of you. The first step is submitting to God and then watching what He will do.

GOING DEEPER

REFLECTION

1. Have you been avoiding dealing with trauma in your life?

2. Pride is a sin present in our human nature, and one of its effects is to disconnect us from God and convince us we don't need anyone. How might pride be stopping you from moving out of trauma?

3. Are there any areas where you are refusing to submit to God as your loving Father?

4. What signs has God given you to encourage you to face the pain and frustration of that trauma?

DECREE

Then if my people who are called by my name will humble themselves and pray and seek my face and turn from their wicked ways, I will hear from heaven and will forgive their sins and restore their land. (2 Chronicles 7:14) And he gives grace generously. As the Scriptures say, "God opposes the proud but gives grace to the humble." So humble yourselves before God. Resist the devil, and he will flee from you. (James 4:6–7)

PRAYER

Father, I want to be on a firm foundation. The traumas of my life have left me wounded and hurting. I give them to You and ask for Your Helper, Holy Spirit, to lead me through the healing process. I take responsibility for myself, and I want to learn how to live in the Kingdom of God while I am here on earth. My life is Yours; help me be who You created me to be. In Jesus' name. Amen.

FURTHER READING

Matthew 5–7

1 Peter 5:5–11

The Holy Spirit—An Introduction by John Bevere with Addison Bevere, Messenger International, 2013

The Secret to Kingdom Life by Rick Ciaramitaro, Rick Ciaramitaro, 2011

CHAPTER THREE

THE FOG OF DECEPTION

About three weeks after the crash, my whole family, including me, was scheduled to go to a leadership conference in the city for three days. Since I couldn't really stay by myself —at least the family didn't seem to think I could—I packed my bags too. We were scheduled to go on a bus, but Dave thought it might be nicer for me to ride in our new vehicle. I was up early and getting ready, excited about going, when suddenly I had dizziness and disorientation that were so bad I was almost down and out on the floor. Thank goodness I hit the bed instead. As I stood there shivering, wrapped in a towel with Dave holding me, reality hit me.

"I don't want to play car accident anymore," I cried.

I didn't want to go anywhere or do anything ... certainly not ride three hours in a car and then sit for hours and end up sleeping in a strange bed. But alas, things were out of my control. Little did I know it was just the beginning of the loss of this elusive thing called "control."

The conference came and went. It was difficult, but I survived. I'm sure I learned something, and on top of that, I began to feel some measure of normalcy returning.

Time moved on, ready or not, and my life began to revolve around doctor appointments, physiotherapy, and exercises at home, all of which were meant to help me but ended up working against what my body really needed—rest, and plenty of it. Before this all happened, my husband had planned a business trip to Costa Rica for two weeks. I was to accompany him. I checked with my doctor, and she agreed that two weeks away would be good for me. Bags were packed and we headed off for an adventure. It was a great resting time for me, and my body felt so good in the hot, humid weather. It was their rainy season, and the weather definitely agreed with me. I felt so good when I came back, I thought it would be a good idea to return to work on a gradual basis. Now I wonder if I was insane.

I was a dental assistant and enjoyed my job. My doctor reluctantly agreed to let me try to work. My family thought I knew what I was doing, and the people at physiotherapy didn't really know me enough to put up a fuss, so off to work I went. This was the real beginning of the end of me. Of course, I didn't know that then. I placed all my worth and identity in what I did, so I equated my complete healing with getting back to work full-time. This would mean things would be back to the way they were before this nightmare started. Things would be normal again, and I'd be back to living the dream.

I started working two half days a week, did physiotherapy and home exercises, and made meals. I was in pain and tired all the time, and I kept pushing down inside the anger I was feeling. Time waits for no one. We either use time to our advantage or it will consume us and we'll waste it, wondering where it went. By the fall I was working and struggling with pain, not really knowing what was happening to my body. My insurance company contacted me for what they called an "assessment." Up to this point they had been great, giving me a cleaning allowance and paying me the difference in my wages for the time I couldn't work.

They sent an assessor to my home to do three hours of testing. I was on my best behaviour and was pleasant to the man. After all, my insurance company was for me and not against me, right? After almost two months the report came through, and it stated that I was recovered and could return to work full-time. I was devastated, because I was currently working three mornings a week, and I physically couldn't do more. We had a mortgage and two car payments, as well as bills like everyone else, and we weren't in a position to have my income cut by two thirds and take on the expenses for cleaning. After much soul searching and confusion, I contacted my doctor. She set them straight about my recovery and insisted that I couldn't possibly return to full-time employment. Unfortunately, the seed was planted, and I thought I had to get moving and help my recovery along, so I added another morning and was now working four half days.

At the end of 2008, nine months after my accident and with the scare of being hung out to dry by my insurance company, along with extra stress to my body, my doctor suggested that it would be in my best interest to consider contacting a lawyer. Happy New Year! I remembered two large law firms from when I worked at an insurance company in my younger days. I wrote them down, asked Dave to pick one, placed a phone call, and from that point on was in the big leagues, so to speak. For the first time in my life, I had legal representation to speak for me and protect me from the big, bad insurance company.

Even though my insurance company had a responsibility to legally help me, I found out they weren't really for me. This began a walk into a world I knew existed but had been fortunate enough to avoid up to this time in my life. This was a world where professional people assured me that they knew more about me than I did. Truth be told, they were very convincing. They handed out the same diagnosis over the course of more than thirty assessments. I was healed. They were baffled as to why I wasn't improving and insisted I should be doing better.

Meanwhile, the muscles in my shoulders and upper back would not relax ... could not relax. When I turned my head, I felt disoriented, and when my arms were held up for more than a minute, they made my neck hurt. I was banging into doorways, and if I looked at something for any length of time, I felt nauseated. I was forced to adapt by turning my body as one unit from head to waist. I was confused, putting things in odd places, and sometimes had a blank look on my face when someone asked me a question. I was in pain constantly and filled with an anger that I continually stuffed down. I was still working and thought I was functioning quite well, as long as I didn't have to learn anything new. But when I came home I couldn't seem to get any meaningful rest, and I got next to nothing done.

During this season, I had no clue of all that was going on inside of me. I was unaware of anything but the pain my body was giving me, and I remember the tiredness. I was tired all the time. It's amazing how familiar you can become with ailments, accepting them as normal very quickly.

In the spring of the following year, the physiotherapy clinic released me and said they couldn't do anything else for me. At that point I was only going there to do the exercises, and I could do them at home. I continued to go to massage therapy, which brought temporary relief. I wasn't really looking for relief—I wanted answers. My massage therapist was very encouraging, telling me not to give up ... to keep searching, and I would find the help I needed.

I had an injury I couldn't explain, my mind was working against me, and I was in denial that anything was wrong. The crazy thing about it all was that I appeared normal from the outside—how I moved, how I responded. Because I was convinced I was getting better, I could convince most of the people around me that I actually was. I've been told I am an influencer, which is good if you're using your influence for the right cause. It's much like any gift we have—we can use it for what it was made to be used for, or for our own selfish reasons. You can only fool yourself for so long before it catches up to you. And it did catch up.

Upon saying goodbye to physiotherapy, I read online that Pilates is very beneficial to individuals with my type of injury. I was approved by my insurance company for some classes, so I joined up and added this to my regime of exercises. Remember, I believed that exercising these sore muscles would help them heal. Just to clear up a few things ... at this point, I didn't realize how hard I'd hit my head. Unfortunately, the wrong mindset of "the more I do the more I'll heal" was in full gear. There are a lot of things I didn't know back then. I was in survival mode—it's called, "fight or flight." It isn't in my nature to take flight, so I fought and hoped for the best.

I went to the city twice a week to a class where I was told to take it easy and do what I could. That was like setting a bone in front of a dog and saying, "Just lick that bone, don't chew." I jumped in and was doing everything with everyone else. The thought of it now doesn't sit well with me, and I realize how messed up I was. The owner of the club obviously saw that I wasn't doing well and mentioned the name of a physiotherapist who dealt with chronic pain patients. She gave me her number and said I should call her to talk. I didn't call right away. I don't remember how many classes I went to, but exercise was definitely one of the straws that broke this camel's back.

DRIVEN TO DOING

Strive:
1. to devote serious effort or energy;
2. to struggle in opposition.

A picture is worth a thousand words, but I don't have a picture of what I looked like at this stage of my journey, climbing out from under the curse of striving. While it may be written in only a few pages, this period actually took up a whole year of my life. I was in extreme pain every day. Looking back, I may have felt I was doing all this by myself, but if God had not been with me, I don't think I would have survived. Deception will do that to you. I based my value on what I could accomplish, and I'd put myself in quite a tight spot. My body needed rest, but I wouldn't allow it to rest.

Wrong beliefs that I had been acting on for years were not going away because I needed to rest. Personal change comes with a price. We cannot wish change to happen. When circumstances are standing in front of us like a mountain, we usually want to go around that obstacle when God wants us to go over it to conquer it. When we reach the top ... oh my, that feeling of victory is sweet! There's nothing like the feeling of real accomplishment, a more-than-conqueror feeling.

When we operate under the veil of deception, we cannot see properly. We see through the filter of the stronghold that has set itself up in our minds. When we face circumstances, we see the solution to the problem through that same filter. What we think is the way out is really another trek around the same destructive cycle. That's what I discovered through striving to make myself better. I was thinking I could heal myself! Really? Who did I think I was ... God?

All my life I'd been independent. I could do everything myself. I might let you help me, but I really didn't need your help, and I liked things done my way. God wanted to show me that I needed Him. Because I'd always done everything my way, it wasn't going to be as easy as it sounded to submit to God's way. In order to know God's way, I had to get to know God. I thought I had to do things perfectly. I knew I wasn't perfect. I didn't think I was worth anything at all, but if I performed well and did things just right, that would make up for my worthlessness. What a damaging way of thinking.

On my journey of getting to know God, I learned I was made in His image—I was a child of God. If it was true that He had all these wonderful characteristics, then maybe I could learn to be like my Father in Heaven, and maybe I wasn't as worthless as I thought. It's freeing to learn you are wrong, especially when your thoughts are negative and condescending towards yourself. It's freeing to know you can replace those thoughts with what God says about you—the truth of who you are in Christ.

The pride in me pushed me to constantly do more and more, putting me on a destructive path that I could not devote the energy to anymore. I was like a hamster on a wheel of destruction, going round and round, and I didn't know how to stop. I don't think I even thought about asking God to help me stop. I was enveloped in striving to perform ... and it was serious business. The enemy named pride was out to kill, steal, and destroy my life again, and I was just going along for the ride. I didn't feel there was a way out, but the truth was the very opposite. I went through this trauma so I could tell you there is hope. You can have victory. You don't have to stay on the wheel of destructive behaviour. God has a plan for you, one with a future and a hope (Jeremiah 29:11).

To change, we only need to repent. Repentance means that we're saying, "I agree with you, God—this is wrong. I'm sorry. Please forgive me and cleanse me of this sin that is keeping me from You. Show me what I'm missing of Your nature." Repentance means we change the way we think, and then our actions follow. How easy is that? Religion has made God complicated. Jesus said those who call upon His name shall be saved (Romans 10:13). Call on His name, agree with God that you were wrong, receive forgiveness, and ask "What am I missing from You?" Then talk to Holy Spirit and He will help you to walk a new walk. That's what repentance is about. The simplicity of the Kingdom of God is yours. Take that step of faith.

GOING DEEPER

REFLECTION

1. Personal change comes with a price. Write down the next step you need to take in your road to recovery. What are the costs involved?

2. You are a child of God. Where do you see yourself trying to strive or earn this truth instead of simply believing it?

3. Ask Holy Spirit to reveal any destructive cycles in your life. Write them down and believe that God is at work in those cycles.

4. What is the truth about your situation according to God? Look in the Bible for some verses that speak to you about your situation. You can hold on to these promises as you continue to move forward.

DECREE

By Your words I can see where I'm going; they throw a beam of light on my dark path. I've committed myself and I'll never turn back from living by your righteous order. Everything's falling apart on me, God; put me together again with your Word. Festoon me with Your finest sayings, God; teach me your holy rules. My life is as close as my own hands, but I don't forget what you have revealed. The wicked do their best to throw me off track, but I don't swerve an inch from your course. I inherited your book on living; it's mine forever—what a gift! And how happy it makes me! I concentrate on doing exactly what you say—I always have and always will. (Psalm 119:105–112, MSG)

PRAYER

Jesus, I repent of the pride and fear that keeps me locked in the cycles that are destroying me, killing this life You have given me. I need Your loving kindness to help me understand me. Will You come into my circumstance like a mighty rushing wind and gather up all the scattered pieces of my life? I want to change the way I think about You and myself. I want to know You and want to know who You made me to be. Teach me Your ways. Amen.

FURTHER READING

Titus 3:3–11

1 Corinthians 6:9–11

Victory over the Darkness by Neil T. Anderson, Regal Books, 1990 (First Edition), Neil T. Anderson, 2000 (Second Edition)

Victory over the Darkness Study Guide by Neil T. Anderson, Gospel Light, 1994, 2000

CHAPTER FOUR

THE BLACK HOLE

One year and three months after my car accident, and one year after starting back to work, I had a body breakdown. I felt completely and utterly hopeless and totally defeated. It's something you only understand if you've been there—that unexplainable place of total and complete despair with no vision for anything. You feel like death would be a relief from the pain. Thank God He surrounded me with people who loved and supported me and that I had enough sense left to reach out and be honest with someone. By this point I had a mentor and had been seeing her every other week since becoming a born-again believer. She always stood with me, proving over and over again that she was for me while continuing to deposit invaluable wisdom that I had the choice to put into practice. Wisdom is an action word. If you have it, you must use it for it to be of any benefit to yourself and others.

I'm dodging the subject here. To be honest, dodging is something I do when it gets painful for me, and this is where the real story begins. Up to this point, I was in denial. Persons in denial are dangerous to themselves and others if they let deception continue and refuse to deal with reality. The reality of my situation was before me, and I had a choice to make—accept reality, or continue in the deception and die a slow, painful death inside while remaining a shell of a person, bitter and resentful for things I couldn't change. Live in the past, or move forward. It seems like a simple choice now, but at that time it was a huge mountain—and I was at the bottom looking straight up. A door had closed on the day of my car accident, and it had taken me over a year for the reality of that closed door to catch up with me. I had to accept the fact that my life was never going to be the same.

Funny how our real-life story seems to begin when we get to the end of ourselves and realize we cannot do it anymore ... that something has to change. That's good news, because when we realize we're at the bottom of the pit, God can reveal Himself to us. Truth says all who call upon the name of the Lord shall be saved (Romans 10:13). Saved I was, but I still had to walk through the process, and it certainly wasn't the way I thought it should go.

I dropped into the chair at my appointment with my mentor and started crying. I couldn't stop. My mentor later told me that she wished I could have seen my own face. I'm glad she didn't tell me on that fateful day. If I could have seen it, I might have died on the spot. That's what I felt like doing—from my perspective, anyway. I hadn't slept for weeks, my muscles were constantly aching (probably the mega-exercising didn't help), and my head was constantly swirling with thoughts. I couldn't rest physically, spiritually, or emotionally. I was a mess. I'm so grateful for her and so glad I took her wisdom that day and used it. She showed me I needed to make some changes, right then and there, if I wanted to move forward. The die had been cast. What would I do ... sink or swim?

First, I talked to my employer of almost twenty years and cut back on my hours. Second, I called the physiotherapist recommended by my Pilates teacher and made an appointment to talk to her in more depth. I didn't realize at that point that she was a divine connection. God set me up. Even when I didn't see it, He was taking good care of me and had only the best for me—she was the best in her field.

At our first meeting, she read me like a book, telling me there were definitely some things wrong. She wasn't too specific, so that she wouldn't scare me away. She could see I wasn't in a good place. I didn't come to her for relief, although the fact remained that I was a ball of pain. Even though I couldn't tell her where it hurt, or use the infamous pain scale of one to ten, she knew I was after complete deliverance from the pain.

In my walk of following the Lord, I learned not to ask for relief; instead, I've always wanted to have the root issue dealt with in my heart. Relief was never enough for me. I thank God for that tenacity, because I'd need it in the years to follow. I had tasted considerable freedom in my life before my car accident, and I knew the benefits of walking without chains, but I still had some strong shackles to deal with. I had tasted and seen that the Lord was good (Psalm 34:8). The world had certainly left me to my own resources, so I trusted God and kept pushing forward as much as I could.

After discussing some issues with me, my therapist put me on a table, felt around a bit, and told me I'd be fine ... it would just take time. Then she did two wonderful things—she told me to put away my weights, and she gave me a neck heating pad. For most people, this would seem a ridiculous thing to be thankful for, but when I got home and put that heating pad around my neck and pushed the button, it was like being in Heaven. My neck relaxed, the pain subsided quicker and better than with any drug I'd ever tried, and I felt like a human being for twenty minutes. After it turned off and I proceeded to get up, I felt very dizzy and my head felt weird. The heat had released my muscles, and immediately symptoms of the deeper issues I would be dealing with started to surface. That's about the time the headaches began to intensify. The process had begun, and so far, I was not a big fan.

Cutting back on my hours did bring some relief, but my body wasn't in agreement, and I kept getting worse. The pain in my neck, and the headaches, became a large issue. A decision had to be made, and no one would tell me what to do. I went to see my doctor, whom I'd been seeing all along, and while she encouraged me, she wouldn't make the decision for me to stop working. I had to slam that door shut myself and lock it. Looking back, it's a good thing I made that decision, as I'd have no one to blame—and neither would the insurance companies.

In the late summer of that year, I told my boss that I was leaving and not coming back to work in the foreseeable future. That may seem insignificant to some people, and some would even be happy to leave their place of employment forever, but I had worked in the same office for almost twenty years with the same three people, knee to knee and head to head on some occasions. We knew each other well and were a working family.

I'm a people person. I loved the clients that came in, and I loved helping some of them deal with difficult procedures they had to go through when they came to the dentist. Side note here: on the list of places most people would rather not go, funerals, lawyers, and dentists are at the top. Funerals are inevitable in our lives, and depending where the deceased person is going, are bearable. Lawyers? I was going to find out about them in just a few months. I didn't mind dentists. I loved my job, and I was giving up something I loved for an unknown future. Sounds easy, doesn't it? Read on.

In hindsight, I can see that my whole life revolved around working. Whether at a place of employment or at home, I was occupied doing something from sun up to sundown, because it made me feel good about myself. Performance was the real issue, the root of the problem. I had pushed my body over the edge, and it couldn't recover because I couldn't stop "doing" long enough to relax. So I stopped working.

My last day was the beginning of a two-week office shut down, and I actually enjoyed that time off. When it was time for the office to open and I didn't go back to work, reality slapped me in the face. I sat in my recliner (compliments of my insurance company) and cried for eight hours every day for two weeks. It would start as soon as the last person was out the door of our home until the first person arrived home after work. I'd try to pull myself together to make dinner. I fell into depression, not so much that everyone knew, but it was there. I was good at covering up things that I didn't want anyone to know about ... a great pretender, actually. But I didn't fool my mentor, Pastor C., or my physiotherapist, Diane. They had been given eyes to see the extent of what was happening and asked the right questions.

Diane suggested that I see a psychologist for insurance purposes so they would know what was going on. At that point I was done arguing. I made up my mind to continue seeing her after the first visit, as I believed she'd do the best she knew to help me. I submitted to her wisdom and followed her instructions.

One day I found a card in my wallet that I'd picked up at a women's conference a couple of years earlier. I thought I'd keep it if I ever had a friend who needed some help. If I was on my cell phone, I'd insert a rolling-on-the-floor-with-laughing smiley face, because who would ever have thought I would be the person in need of a counsellor for depression? I called the name on the card, and she said she couldn't help me, but gave me the name of someone who could.

I connected with the psychologist she suggested and had an assessment with her. I was now officially nuts—or at least that's what I thought at the time. I was confronted on every side. I was seeing a psychologist every two weeks and Pastor C. the weeks I didn't see the psychologist, with phone calls and emails between visits. Let's not forget Diane, my physiotherapist, who didn't let up either. God had His eye on me during that period, and He knew what I needed and provided me with the best so I could keep moving forward.

I didn't sleep well, and that wasn't helping my recovery, but I did discover that certain things helped. The donut shaped pillow I made protected the back of my head from touching the pillow. If my head did touch the pillow, I'd experience a quick, brutal nausea. I lay on a large heating pad that covered my shoulders and back. I slept in my recliner, and Dave got the new king-size bed, which my occupational therapist had requested from the insurance company, to himself.

When my occupational therapist found out I wasn't sleeping on the bed because I couldn't lie flat, she got us adjustable beds, one for Dave and one for me. Not too often a person gets two beds purchased for them, but I needed it, and God provided. After I got used to the bed, I loved it. I changed positions so much each night that I had the markings worn off my remote after the first three months. Sleep was still an issue, and the headaches were getting a little more intense. If I had a good night's rest and stayed in one spot for too long, my head would ache the next day. If I moved around all night, I was exhausted the next day. Quite a cycle to be in. To top it off, I was also battling to stay above the effects of depression.

Of all the different stages of my recovery, this was the hardest and the most serious test of my faith in God. After I pushed through, I had no doubt that God was watching over me and protecting me, and was my ever-present help whenever I needed Him. Thank God, because it was a very "depressing" time, for lack of a better word. I'd wake up in the morning and not want to get up, but I did. Once I'd get up, I'd be so tired, I could barely function.

After the initial two weeks of crying every day, I was spent. I would cry more occasionally, once or twice a day, instead of all day. The crying eventually subsided, and I entered into a resignation that this was where I was at. I'd push myself to brush my teeth in the morning, but at night I'd hear in my head: "Why bother? Who cares about washing your face; brush your teeth in the morning." I was a dental assistant for goodness' sake—I had to brush my teeth. I'd do it and it would feel like I was brushing through three feet of heavy snow. It makes my eyes well up thinking about that time, because by nature I'm a fighter. I rarely give up when something is worth fighting for, but this was one of the most hopeless times I'd ever experienced. It was a period of letting go of my previous life, the death of my old self. As I look back on it, I can't quite recall how I made it through.

Let's get real here—I know it was God's grace that kept me going. Sometimes ten minutes at a time was all I could focus on ... some days, a minute at a time. I did focus, with the help of good people to support and encourage me. I know I wouldn't be where I am today unless I chose to trust those around me to lead, guide, and direct when I was so messed up that I couldn't put two and two together. There are those people we encounter in life who pretend they care about us, but they give up when the going gets tough, or they don't know how to deal with what's going on, because they're too focused on their own issues. They're more worried about how it's all going to affect them than how they can actually help. But there are also those who do care and dare to speak the truth when you need to hear it. Those are your true friends. They care enough to give you that push you need to move forward. God will always put someone in your path who will be a true friend; you must choose whether to receive that friendship or not. I've been fortunate enough to have several friends who did that for me, some of whom were in my life for a short time, while others are still walking with me.

FROM DENIAL TO DEPRESSION

> Depression: a serious medical condition in which a person feels very sad, hopeless, and unimportant and often is unable to live in a normal way.

When the fog of deception that keeps you in denial is found out and you walk into the clearing of your senses, it can be a shock to your system. My body's system was definitely messed up, because I had pushed it over its physical limits. I found out that I had been running on full adrenaline output for an entire year. My body couldn't keep up with the physical demands I'd placed on it. It collapsed, and I was barely able to function.

One might wonder what I was thinking—how an intelligent, reasonable, sane woman could do that to herself. It's amazing how our bodies are made and how much abuse they can take. This is a warning: abuse will catch up with you sooner or later. Who knows what might have happened had I done things differently? I probably could have avoided a lot of steps in my journey. I do have regrets about how I handled myself, but I also believe God has the best for those who love Him, even though we don't always understand how tragedy, trauma, and pain can end up being for our good. It's how we handle those situations that matter—our attitude when faced with difficulties.

I don't have to expand too much about bad attitudes. We all have them at some point. Maybe for you it's once a day, or maybe you're blessed and it's only once a year, but we do have them. After all, we are human.

Every one of us has had bad experiences in life. I've already mentioned this, and you probably wouldn't have read this far if you didn't agree with some of what I've written. Our attitude determines how we will maneuver through a day. If we wake up with a chip on our shoulder and think the world is out to get us, most likely that's how we'll see the rest of our day. An attitude adjustment will flip our vision to see the good in people and the beauty of the world around us. We don't want to ignore the bad, but choose to be thankful for what we have and for those we are blessed to have in our life.

During the worst of my days, the only thing I had control over was my attitude. I got into the habit of speaking these thoughts out loud: "I choose to thank you, God, for this day; I can breathe, I can move my body parts, I can think." Some days when the world seemed to be closing in on me, I didn't speak out loud my thankfulness and gratitude; on those days, I couldn't see the good in anything. My only advice in hindsight is to practice thanking God every day for something, and then when the trials hit, you'll have this habit firmly in place. No matter what you go through, there's only one thing you have control over, and that's your attitude. Next time you're feeling life has let you down, check your bad attitude at the door of your heart before it gets inside. Your life will improve exponentially!

Depression is nasty. I know there are different medical conditions that contribute to clinical depression, but I didn't have that type. I can only comment on the depression I went through. It focuses on the circumstance and causes you to fold into yourself. Some days I can feel it trying to sneak up on me and latch on, but I've gotten freedom from it, and I know the symptoms. It wants me to focus on the hopelessness of my current situation and all the "cannots" in my life instead of the "can dos." I have a choice to check my attitude and be thankful for what I have instead of what I don't have.

Depression makes you feel like you're all alone: "No one knows what you suffer; no one cares about you and how you feel." Have you ever heard those words? They aren't your thoughts—they're the words of satan being spoken into your mind. He wants you to come into agreement with him and fall into the self-pity of depression. You are not alone ... ever. God is always watching over you, waiting for you to acknowledge Him. Being thankful acknowledges God. He doesn't need you to be thankful for His benefit; it's for your benefit. If you're thanking someone, you're acknowledging their presence and their importance to you. When you acknowledge God's presence, the atmosphere of death and destruction dissipates, because God is everywhere. He surrounds us, and when we thank Him for what He's done, we show that we actually believe He is real. Once you use your voice, something happens and you feel better. You've told your soul, "It's okay; God's right here."

GOING DEEPER

REFLECTION

1. Are there areas in your life where others would say you're living in denial? Sometimes it's painful to look at this, but it's an important step in moving out of trauma and into wholeness.

2. Exercise: If you're unsure if you're living in denial, ask someone you trust to give their input, and then take what they say to Holy Spirit. Ask Him to confirm what's true.

3. Do you have a bad attitude towards a person or situation in your life?

4. Can you identify with depression? Write down what it feels like, sounds like, looks like. Take each of these areas and line them up with the truth of the Word of God. What does He say about each area? What is He bringing you out of and into?

DECREE

Listen to this prayer of mine, God; pay attention to what I'm asking. Answer me—you're famous for your answers! Do what's right for me. But don't, please don't, haul me into court; not a person alive would be acquitted there. The enemy hunted me down; he kicked me and stomped me within an inch of my life. He put me in a black hole, buried me like a corpse in that dungeon. I sat there in despair, my spirit draining away, my heart heavy, like lead. I remembered the old days, went over all you've done, pondered the ways you've worked, stretched out my hands to you, as thirsty for you as a desert thirsty for rain. Hurry with your answer, God! I'm nearly at the end of my rope. Don't turn away; don't ignore me! That would be certain death. If you wake me each morning with the sound of your loving voice, I'll go to sleep each night trusting in You. Point out the road I must travel; I'm all ears, all eyes before you. Save me from my enemies, God—you're my only hope! Teach me how to live to please you, because you're my God. Lead me by your blessed Spirit into cleared and level pastureland. Keep up your reputation, God—give me life! In your justice, get me out of this trouble! In your great love, vanquish my enemies; make a clean sweep of those who harass me. And why? Because I'm your servant. (Psalm 143, MSG) I bless God every chance I get; my lungs expand with his praise. I live and breathe God; if things aren't going well, hear this and be happy:

Join me in spreading the news; together let's get the word out. God met me more than halfway, he freed me from my anxious fears. Look at him; give him your warmest smile. Never hide your feelings from him. When I was desperate, I called out, and God got me out of a tight spot. God's angel sets up a circle of protection around us while we pray. Open your mouth and taste, open your eyes and see—how good God is. Blessed are you who run to him. Worship God if you want the best; worship opens doors to all his goodness. Young lions on the prowl get hungry, but God-seekers are full of God. Come, children, listen closely; I'll give you a lesson in God worship. Who out there has a lust for life? Can't wait each day to come upon beauty? Guard your tongue from profanity, and no more lying through your teeth. Turn your back on sin; do something good. Embrace peace—don't let it get away! God keeps an eye on his friends, his ears pick up every moan and groan. God won't put up with rebels; he'll cull them from the pack. Is anyone crying for help? God is listening, ready to rescue you. If your heart is broken, you'll find God right there; if you're kicked in the gut, he'll help you catch your breath. Disciples so often get into trouble; still, God is there every time. He's your bodyguard, shielding every bone; not even a finger gets broken. The wicked commit slow suicide; they waste their lives hating the good. God pays for each slave's freedom; no one who runs to him loses out. (Psalm 34, MSG)

PRAYER

Thank you, Father, for sending Jesus to die for me and to rescue me from the pit of hell. I need help to see as You see, to be able to receive what You have for me. I want to be a thankful person every day of my life, focusing on good and not evil. Come and change my heart, help me change my attitude and to always be thankful and grateful no matter what circumstances surround me. I pray that You will release peace and joy as I release praises to You. I pray You will take me up to the heavenly places where I can see from Your perspective. I want to know You more, and in turn, I will learn who I truly am as Your son or daughter. Thank You for loving me. In Jesus' name, Amen.

FURTHER READING

Psalm 34

Psalm 145:1–3

The Search for Significance by Robert S. McGee, Thomas Nelson, Inc., 1998, 2003

The Search for Significance Workbook by Robert S. McGee, Life-Way Press, 2004, 2007

Jesus Today (Devotional) by Sarah Young, Thomas Nelson Inc., 2012

CHAPTER FIVE

Coming into Reality

For a few months I sat in my recliner for about eight hours every day, when I wasn't heading to appointments and insurance assessments. I spent my nights trying to sleep in my adjustable bed, constantly adjusting because the pain woke me up if I stayed in one position too long. As I continued to see Diane, she began showing me that I had received more than just the whiplash injury. She sat me down and explained to me that she suspected I had Mild Traumatic Brain Injury. I knew I wasn't functioning as I used to, but the differences were so subtle that I just thought I was a little bit crazy. Here are just a few examples: Even though I could physically turn my head by itself, when my eyes were open, I turned my whole body as one unit from the waist up. I was very bent forward all the time, seeming to be folding into myself instead of standing straighter. Pushing a cart down the aisles at the grocery store made me feel unstable and a little dizzy. I'd bump into people when I was walking beside them, and had some bruises from door jams that always seemed to be in my walking path. My vision would get quite blurry at times. I never told anyone, because these things were all very subtle, and the pain from my shoulders and neck seemed to be more important at the time.

Diane tested me and showed me that when I stood and closed my eyes, I swayed back and forth and I'd end up falling over if I didn't open them. I was more fascinated than shocked. I had my family and friends try this test. I thought it was cool that I finally had something to show everyone. I told every doctor and assessor, because it was something they couldn't deny; it was visible proof that something wasn't right.

I didn't know what Mild Traumatic Brain Injury was, but I didn't like the sound of "brain injury" at all. I couldn't say it for quite some time after that. I did, however, go online to check it out, because I didn't really believe what I'd been told. I discovered that all the things that were happening to me were symptoms of Mild Traumatic Brain Injury. Woe is me! I did not like it— not one little bit. Diane seemed unmoved by the whole thing, and I kept moving along, learning a new way to exercise. Through this period of time, I was still maneuvering through depression, but I could tell that I was beginning to pull out of it. I started to see a small ray of light at the end of that long, dark tunnel. I was too busy going to appointments, learning about myself, and becoming body-aware to sleep all day and focus on the negative.

I started going to Pilates again, but now I had private lessons on a machine. I liked it, because I was able to do something tangible to help myself along. I also went to swimming classes given by Diane, which turned out to be a hoot. I don't swim—I didn't even like the water, and there I was with seven other people all in the same boat as me ... some worse.

The water was eighty-six degrees and felt lovely, even though I felt like a fish out of water. I was in the pool for about ten minutes doing the group exercises, slowly walking in the water, lifting my legs and swirling my arms around slowly, when all of a sudden, I started feeling dizzy. Nausea came upon me, and I thought I was going to pass out and slide down into the bottom of the pool. Diane must have been watching me, waiting for something like that to happen, because she calmly told me to stop and sit down on the steps. I sat and watched the rest of the hour-long class, feeling like a failure but so glad I didn't have to move. The movement of the water had made me feel sick. This little escapade prompted us to do further investigation.

As you've probably gathered, further investigation was a little bit scary for me by now. When you're in a car accident, everything must be approved by the insurance company before you proceed, or they won't pay for treatment. For every treatment I requested, there seemed to be an assessment to go with it. Professionals in their respective fields checked me out and wrote down their findings. I found out that insurance companies didn't like most of Diane's patients, because they didn't have the normal type of injuries. Diane's patients had injuries like Mild Traumatic Brain Injury, for which there were no specific guidelines. Going forward, this made my treatment a little more challenging to tackle.

UNDER COVER

Cover:

1. to guard from attack;
2. to provide protection to or against.

We all learn how important it is to listen to our parents/guardians when we are young. I'm sure we've all heard the words, "I told you so." These words don't sound particularly wonderful when we hear them, but they're probably true, and choosing not to listen likely resulted in trouble. They probably spoke from experience and wisdom, but we all like to be our own person and try it our own way. I did that for most of my life ... doing my own thing, going my own way.

I was a mess by the time I was in my forties. I had no boundaries, and did things the way I wanted. My family didn't know what to expect from me, because there was no predictability. I would suppress all my emotions and then blow up at something very small. It was ridiculous when I think about it now.

I started the discipleship/mentorship program offered at my church shortly after becoming a Christian. I had no idea what was expected of me or what was required of me to grow, but I knew I didn't want to stay the way I was. There is a deception when you come into the family of God that all will be well, and everything will take care of itself. All was not well for me. After the initial joy at the realization there was a Heaven and I was headed there, I discovered that family situations didn't improve much, and I still reacted the same way. The only difference was that I'd suddenly feel ashamed of my behaviour. Coming under the cover of a spiritual mentor helped me change some of my attitudes and grow and mature. Most importantly, it helped me to find my way to the presence of God by clearing out all the clutter in my mind. I learned how to be real with God through being real with my mentor. Discipleship/mentorship is a necessity for living the Kingdom of God on earth. There are no shortcuts.

I'm not sure about you, but when I'm told something I don't want to hear, usually I want to run away—perhaps not physically, but certainly mentally. I think part of this arises from being motivated by fun. Dealing with issues is never fun, but the freedom that comes with the healing of my heart is pretty great. It's part of changing our perspective back to the positive—the full life God intended us to live.

Being under cover doesn't only apply to mentoring relationships, but also to whomever is placed in authority over you. I have given several people authority in the past and will continue to throughout my life. I understand that God has placed these people in authority over my life for a specific reason. It places me under their cover, and since God placed them in my life, I remain ultimately under His cover and protection.

First and foremost, I was placed under my husband's cover when we got married. It's a wonderful feeling to be protected, and I know God speaks to him about what's best for our family and marriage. Years ago, I didn't appreciate or understand what that meant, but with help, I do now. When I placed myself under the authority of my physiotherapist and decided to do what she suggested, I truly believe that God gave her wisdom to help me move forward. I also came under the covering of my lawyer, my doctor, my chiropractor, and my craniosacral therapist (who is yet to be introduced in the story). God put me in touch with those He had handpicked to help me, and He was able to release wisdom specifically for me through them. Upon reflection, I can see where His hand was on everything.

The order of authority is part of the way in which the Kingdom of God functions. I can only have authority when I place myself under authority. I tried it on my own, and that didn't work very well. Getting under cover is actually submission to God and admitting you need help, and that's okay. We all need each other. We're all connected, and when we get under cover and get real, God can really begin to move in our lives.

GOING DEEPER

REFLECTION

1. What is your general attitude concerning authority figures?

2. Describe your relationship with specific authority figures in your life.

3. What experiences with authority have shaped your current view?

4. Ask the Holy Spirit to show you any areas in your life where you are resistant to submitting to authority.

5. Is there anyone who was or is an authority figure that you need to forgive?

6. What steps do you need to take to begin moving towards being able to submit?

DECREE

Oh, the joys of those who do not follow the advice of the wicked, or stand around with sinners, or join in with mockers. But they delight in the law of the Lord, meditating on it day and night. They are like trees planted along the riverbank, bearing fruit each season. Their leaves never wither, and they prosper in all they do. (Psalm 1:1–3) Obey your spiritual leaders, and do what they say. Their work is to watch over your souls, and they are accountable to God. Give them reason to do this with joy and not with sorrow. That would certainly not be for your benefit. (Hebrews 13:17) A good tree produces good fruit, and a bad tree produces bad fruit. A good tree can't produce bad fruit, and a bad tree can't produce good fruit. So every tree that does not produce good fruit is chopped down and thrown into the fire. Yes, just as you can identify a tree by its fruit, so you can identify people by their actions. (Matthew 7:17–20)

PRAYER

Jesus, I want to live a full life. I need help to get out of the destructive cycles I'm in. I want to get under the cover of someone who has gone before me and knows the way! Please direct me to someone I can trust, someone whom I can follow as they follow You. I want to get real and come out of the places I hide when I'm afraid. I want to walk in love and peace. I want to influence my world for the Kingdom of God. In Jesus' name I pray. Amen.

FURTHER READING

2 Timothy 2:1–7

Luke 7:1–10

Matthew ~~38~~ 28:16–20

Under Cover by John Bevere, Thomas Nelson Inc., 2001

Spiritual Slavery to Spiritual Sonship by Jack Frost, Destiny Image Publishers Inc., 2006

CHAPTER SIX

BOUNDARIES ARE GOOD

I was getting all sorts of revelations about myself and learning to be "body aware," as Diane called it. I also learned how to practically apply everything I was receiving. Even though I had the best professionals around me to give me wise advice, I always struggled with whether I wanted to do what they advised.

During one of our meetings, Pastor C. suggested I read a book on boundaries that came with a workbook. I didn't want to read it at that time, so I said I'd think about it. It seemed like a lot to do. I was coming out from under depression, and I'm no fool—in my life there was no such thing as reading a book and doing a workbook unless I was willing to make changes.

God knew what I needed. My next appointment with my psychologist was at a newly renovated office in her house. As we were discussing me, I saw a copy of the same book staring me in the face from right behind her head. I couldn't keep my eyes off it, and—surprise—at my next appointment with Pastor C., I asked for the book and the workbook. It has been said that great minds think alike. It turned out that my psychologist and Pastor C. had known each other for years. Imagine that!

I can truthfully say that using that book and following the principles in it has changed my life for the better. We are all of great value, and boundaries in our lives are put in place to keep us safe. We are worth keeping safe. If you don't believe that, I know where you can get a good book that will change the way you think about boundaries! It's listed under further reading at the end of this chapter. Boundaries are very freeing. I stay in mine and I respect others'. As a result, others learn to respect mine and everyone gets along just fine—most of the time.

When I started implementing boundaries, I was very angry, which the book assured me was normal. I was angry because it became apparent that I needed to start asking for help in areas I didn't want to. These were normal, everyday things I used to do myself before the accident that now I was too stubborn and prideful to ask for help for. I did want to change in my heart, so with some coaching, I tried asking for help nicely ... even though I was burning mad inside. My family was more than willing to help me in any area I asked, but it was an internal issue for me. This was something I had to work through, and while it did get easier, even now it still irks me sometimes when I know I need to ask for help. After all, that's what I used to do—I did everything for everyone, and it made me feel really good about myself.

I was now left face to face with myself, and I didn't like what I saw. Everything I did was done to make me feel good and to please everyone around me. I was a performance-approval addict. It wasn't life as usual anymore, and I was going to have to learn how to do things differently—outwardly and inwardly. I needed a mindset change.

As my occupational therapist, Pilates instructor, and physiotherapist showed me a new way to sweep the floor, exercise, and stretch, my mentor and psychologist showed me how to implement boundaries and change the way I thought about myself by renewing my mind with biblical truth. Both seemed to work parallel with each other, and slowly but surely, things started to improve.

I seemed to have some anger issues that didn't originate from the accident but were surfacing because of the accident. My psychologist gave me an anger workbook that helped me face my anger and deal with it instead of stuffing it down and then exploding. Working with Pastor C., I learned that there are more emotions than simply being angry and being happy. Imagine that! I realized that most of the time I wasn't angry at all; I was hurt or sad or in pain, and all those emotions erupted as anger, because I hadn't just stuffed my anger down all those years, but every emotion. No wonder for so many years I felt dead—I was emotionally dead.

While I was learning about the emotional side of myself, Diane was teaching me to be body-aware, which meant listening to how my body spoke to me and told me how it felt. I thought I was doing nothing in those days, but I was in boot camp for learning about myself. I learned so much about me for that year and a half—more than I'd learned the previous fifty years of my life. I was starting to see a glimpse of the woman God had made me to be, and I liked what I saw. This was only the beginning of what I would learn.

My days were full with Pilates, the pool, meetings with Pastor C. and the psychologist, and going to assessments once a month. I had a full-time job looking after me. All the years of ignoring myself and only looking outward had caught up with me. This seemed to be the time to take inventory and fix what needed to be fixed.

Diane did her investigating and was concerned about the issues I had with my balance. As we worked on opening up my shoulders and standing a little straighter, more symptoms popped up. I appeared to be getting worse, although I was assured these symptoms had actually all occurred at that split second of time when I made contact with the car. I had headaches most of the time. I woke up with pain running from the back of my neck up and over the top of my head. The top of my shoulders burned, and I had a stabbing pain in my right shoulder blade almost daily. Any exercise I did was done lying down with my head supported, but still my neck immediately hurt and I felt dizzy.

Diane told me that all exercise that made my neck hurt had to be stopped. This was devastating news to me, because I still believed that if I worked hard at exercising, I could make myself better. She told me I could go to the pool, but I would now go to a pool closer to home, because the insurance company wouldn't pay for me to come to her classes. Here I was—no Pilates and no home exercises, but I could go to the pool that made me feel sick when I looked at the water. Great! I was not impressed with this news at all.

BOUNDARIES

Boundary:

1. imaginary line that shows where an area ends and another area begins;
2. a point or limit that indicates where two things become different;
3. unofficial rules about what should not be done: limits that define acceptable behaviour.

I didn't understand the purpose of boundaries in my life before being taught that they exist to help me. I didn't act with consistency, and basically flew by the seat of my pants through a lot of situations in my life. I lived a very scheduled life and knew what I was doing almost every minute of the day. But within that schedule I had no boundaries in place to regulate my activity, because I didn't much care about myself. I used the schedules as a way to lose myself in the busyness of life. My lack of structure in life didn't serve me well when I couldn't physically do what I wanted after my accident.

Boundaries keep us safe, because we are worth protecting. When we set up boundaries for ourselves of what is acceptable behaviour and what is not, then God can start changing the way we see ourselves. We begin to line up with how He sees us—as precious children who are valuable beyond measure. We are so precious that He sent Jesus to die on a cross so we could have a relationship with our Father in Heaven. Now the choice becomes mine. Will I do my part and set up some boundaries in my life that will protect me because God says I am precious to Him?

Boundaries aren't designed to cage us in, even though we often think this is the case. We instantly get our backs up and think, *No one is going to tell me what to do*. But when you understand that boundaries are designed to protect you, the landscape changes from fences and walls to one of open fields and green pastures, where we can run freely without the worry of being fatally wounded. We may fall within those boundaries, but it's easy to get back up and try again when you know you're in a secure environment.

I was quite good at setting boundaries for others, telling them what they could or could not do. I got quite angry when they didn't co-operate with what I thought they should do. I was a very demanding person, and instead of giving people the opportunity to listen, I commanded them. It didn't work well for me. If you haven't entered the boundary ring, you'll require some help navigating what's healthy for you. Since this isn't a self-help book, ask someone you trust to help you get started.

Once some boundaries had been set up for my physical well-being, I reaped the benefits of having some help completing my day-to-day tasks. I learned how to release the anger to God by asking Holy Spirit to show me why I was angry. I asked Him a lot, and He'd always tell me and then I would repent, if necessary, and ask Him to heal my heart and help me to respond differently.

When we humble ourselves and talk to God (pray), He hear us, answers us, and changes us. Pride keeps us from asking for help from others and from God. When we do ask, we allow God to break down the pride that keeps us from enjoying where we are. Without boundaries in place, we aren't able to enjoy the moment, because we're being controlled by something else, rather than being in control of our own lives. We can be the best God wants us to be, and He will release the best He has for us when we learn to function within the boundaries He gives us. When we're comfortable with those boundaries, He asks us to pull up the stakes and extend our boundaries to the next place He wants us to grow.

That new place may seem smaller, and within the new boundaries it probably is, but when you start functioning in that narrow place, you'll discover more freedom and the ability to function at a higher level than you ever thought you could. When we establish the cycle of boundaries and understand why we have them, we can advance confidently, knowing we are safe and secure in the place He has for us.

GOING DEEPER

REFLECTION

1. What is the purpose of boundaries in someone's life?
2. Do you have a hard time embracing boundaries in your life? Why?
3. Where could adding boundaries in your life help you?
4. In what area(s) do you know you need boundaries right now? What steps can you take?
5. Who can you include in this process to give you guidance, support, and love?

DECREE

Lord, you alone are my inheritance, my cup of blessing. You guard all that is mine. The land you have given me is a pleasant land. What a wonderful inheritance! I will bless the Lord who guides me; even at night my heart instructs me. I know the Lord is always with me. I will not be shaken, for He is right beside me. No wonder my heart is glad, and I rejoice. My body rests in safety. (Psalm 16:5–9) For His divine power reinforces your city gates, blesses your children in the womb. He establishes peace within your borders, fills your markets with hearty golden wheat. (Psalm 147:13–14, VOICE) What's the price of two or three pet canaries? Some loose change, right? But God never overlooks a single one. And He pays even greater attention to you, down to the last detail—even numbering the hairs on your head! So don't be intimidated by all this bully talk. You're worth more than a million canaries. (Luke 12:6–7, MSG)

PRAYER

Holy Spirit, I need a mindset change. I want to walk in the freedom that placing boundaries in my life will bring. Help me to understand that boundaries are to keep me safe. Show me where I need help with boundaries. I want to walk in the wholeness that comes from knowing who You are and knowing who I am. Your Word says that I am valuable, and I will trust You in this area and work with You to bring changes in my life. In Jesus' name I pray. Amen.

FURTHER READING

Psalm 139

John 10:1–10

Matthew 6:28–30

Boundaries by Dr. Henry Cloud and Dr. John Townsend, Yates and Yates, 1992, 2017

Boundaries Workbook by Dr. Henry Cloud and Dr. John Townsend, Yates and Yates, 1995

CHAPTER SEVEN

FACT, FAITH, FEELINGS

In many ways, that year turned out to be a year of discovery. I learned that I had a very complex injury, with many layers to be uncovered. My lawyer joined my support group, sending me to his list of professionals that examined me. At this point, I saw a psychologist, a neurologist, and future care and job specialists—on top of all the assessors I was sent to by my insurance company after Diane requested treatment for the difficulties I was experiencing. I was overwhelmed with the reports coming at me, some confirming I had Mild Traumatic Brain Injury, some stating that something else was wrong, and some stating that I should be doing better by now. I travelled all over Southwestern Ontario to various assessments. It was very discouraging to wait for the reports to come back from some assessments, because I knew by the way they asked the questions that their report wouldn't be favourable. Some of them stated before my appointment that the insurance company only asked them certain questions, so that's all they could answer.

During this period, I listened to the advice given and then talked it over with, and learned to rely on, my support team of professionals instead of those who didn't know me at all. I also learned a very valuable technique that works every time. I was doing a daily devotional designed to change a person's perspective from the now to the eternal value of circumstances. At just the right time when I was beside myself with discouragement from yet another report from another assessor, I read about the three "F's": fact, faith, and feelings (see Further Reading for book reference). It eventually changed the way I looked at a lot of things.

First and foremost, it changed the way I looked at all those medical reports—and there were quite a few. I dreaded getting the mail. I'd see the return address on the envelope and think to myself, *Here I go again*. Before I even opened them, I knew they'd state where I should be in the process of recovery. Every time I read a report like this I'd slip back a couple of steps into a low-grade depression, a kind of melancholy state. Sometimes it would last for a few days, and sometimes for a few weeks.

But the three "F"s changed all that for me. When a report would come, I'd stare at the envelope and say out loud: "I know these pages contain facts, true or not, but I choose to see these words through the eyes of faith. I believe the word of the Lord, and my feelings will come through my faith, not through the facts." This only works if you have faith, of which we have all been given a measure, and if you activate it. You choose to state that what God says in the Bible is true, which means you must trust God. In order to trust Him, you must believe He exists and also that He is a rewarder of those who diligently seek Him (Hebrews 11:6). This has been tried and tested throughout the ages, and now by me too. Fact. Faith. Feelings. Those three words kept depression from slithering back into my life.

DISCOURAGEMENT

Discouragement: a feeling of having lost hope or confidence.

Courage: mental or moral strength to venture, persevere, and with stand danger, fear or difficulty.

We all face discouragement; it's one of satan's well-used weapons. What do we do when discouragement comes in like a flood? We have a choice to make. We can agree with that feeling of hopelessness, or we can take a step of courage and speak the truth to discouragement. It's very real and unavoidable, because discouragement comes from the disappointments in our lives. We all encounter disappointments when we have expectations of others, expectations of the outcomes of situations, and expectations of ourselves. When those expectations aren't met, we can become disappointed. They can be healthy and realistic, but if they don't happen the way we think they should, we get hurt. Undealt with disappointments allow discouragement a place to land.

We can address discouragement quickly and effectively when we place our expectations and our hope in God and what He says about a particular situation. We should stand on the report of the Lord—what the Word of God says—and not what our thoughts or satan is whispering to us. When we remain stuck in discouragement, we move to self-pity (a form of depression), which causes us to fold into ourselves and only see our circumstances, with no way out. This begins a cycle of hopelessness, which can lead to death spiritually and sometimes naturally. God has given us keys to deal with the voice of discouragement before it becomes a destructive cycle.

Disappointment and discouragement run together, but we can separate them and ask God to heal our disappointments and tell discouragement to leave the building. When we acknowledge the facts of any given disappointment, choose to see them through the eyes of faith, and speak the promises of God found in the Bible, our feelings change and line up with God's view of the situation. This is courage, and it activates our faith. God is faithful, and He will not forsake us, but we have our part to play. In this case, our part is using our voice to speak out the truth over the situation. God is good all the time, and He will take the worst situation and turn it into the best if we let Him.

When faced with disappointments:

1. Don't deny the facts. They are real.

2. Choose to see the situation through faith and say it out loud.

3. Take the step of courage. Ask God to heal the disappointment and use scripture to speak the truth.

4. Tell discouragement to go and your feelings to line up with the Word of God.

5. Talk to someone you trust.

Fact. Faith. Feelings. It's so simple, and the results are guaranteed: freedom from discouragement!

GOING DEEPER

REFLECTION

1. What hopeless situation are you facing? Where are you disappointed? Write down some facts about it.

2. Write down how you feel about those the facts.

3. Ask Holy Spirit to show you God's heart concerning this situation. How does He see it? How does He feel about it?

4. Write down God's truth and promises and speak them out loud until faith rises in your heart.

DECREE

God is not a man, so he does not lie. He is not human, so he does not change his mind. Has he ever spoken and failed to act? Has he ever promised and not carried it through? (Numbers 23:19) This is my command—be strong and courageous! Do not be afraid or discouraged. For the LORD your God is with you wherever you go. (Joshua 1:9) Light, space, zest— that's GOD! So, with him on my side I'm fearless, afraid of no one and nothing. (Psalm 27:1, MSG) Don't fret or worry. Instead of worrying, pray. Let petitions and praises shape your worries into prayers, letting God know your concerns. Before you know it, a sense of God's wholeness, everything coming together for good, will come and settle you down. It's wonderful what happens when Christ displaces worry at the center of your life. (Philippians 4:6–7, MSG)

PRAYER

Jesus, I've been disappointed, and discouragement sits at my door. Heal my heart of disappointment. I want to learn how to deal with these expectations that aren't lining up with what You have for me. I want my expectation in You alone. I know I'll still face some disappointments, but I'll run to You for the encouragement, courage, and healing I need to push through to access all You have for me in this lifetime. Jesus, I thank You for the cross which allows me access to all the plans my heavenly Father has predestined for me, which includes hope for the future. Amen.

FURTHER READING

Isaiah 41:10–13

Psalm 31

A Heart to See Forever by Catherine Martin (Devotional), Quiet Time Ministries, 2003

CHAPTER EIGHT

GRACE

Discovering who you really are and learning to like, or dare I say *love* yourself, is not quite as easy as it appears on paper. Years of hating myself and the things I habitually did to further hurt myself and others weren't just going to go away because I didn't want anything to do with them anymore. I had to learn new mindsets and let go of the wrong beliefs I had about myself. I continue to renew my mind daily with what God says about me, and I continue to get revelations of how valuable I am to God. The process, although sometimes a difficult one, is always rewarding. In the end you see what you can become with God at work in you. I understand and agree that no matter the circumstances, God works out all things for my good, because He loves me and I'm His daughter (Romans 8:28).

One of those good things happened when I had the opportunity to go on my first mission trip to Guatemala with a group from my church. To this day, I cannot understand why my doctor released me to go, but bless her that she did, and I went for seven days of glorious heat and further revelations about myself. I discovered what God's grace could enable me to do. It wasn't an easy trip for someone who wasn't able to lift more than ten pounds or do anything physical for more than an hour. Dragging luggage through the airports, onto buses, and into buildings was an adventure for sure. I didn't lift too much, although I did learn that pulling was just as hard on my body as lifting. I went with a great team, and everyone helped me just when I needed it the most.

While we were there, we went to two orphanages and an outreach for alcoholics and prostitutes. We had opportunity to do physical work as well as invest time into the children and people in the surrounding communities. The days went by quickly, and soon it was time to head home. I was so blessed by the people I met there. The places we went were impoverished, and the people living there had practically nothing, as is true with many areas in Central America. Something I heard repeatedly from our group was that although the people were limited in material things, they were so happy to see us—smiles, smiles, and more smiles. There was a language barrier, but we found out that the language of love is the same all over the world.

I realized upon getting back home that there was life beyond the four walls of my house and that I could enjoy life with my limitations when the plans were what God had for me. This trip proved to me that within His plans I would be protected and surrounded by the right people in the right place at the right time to help me accomplish what He has for me to do. What freedom that gave me! I had freedom to enjoy the place where I was, even though it wasn't where I wanted to be. That revelation gave me the opportunity to choose to walk towards contentment, and I could start enjoying each day instead of always waiting for something to change.

AMAZING GRACE

Grace:

1. unmerited divine assistance given humans for their regeneration or sanctification;
2. a virtue coming from God;
3. a state of sanctification enjoyed through divine grace.

Amazing grace ... how sweet that does sound? God gives us divine enablement to accomplish what He has for us to do. I have discovered that grace manifests itself differently for each of us. It's as unique as we are and is individually designed for us. We all need that grace every day to help us live this life in a way that is pleasing to God. When I don't step onto the grace provided for me, I step out on my own path. I believe grace is something we step on and rely on, like standing on the rock of Jesus.

Until I returned from my trip to Guatemala, I didn't understand what had happened to me. I was always waiting for something to change before I was going to do anything worthwhile with my life. I didn't like my new life, because I couldn't like myself or see the path God had set before me. I only saw the path of circumstances, and it led nowhere. Every day became something to endure instead of live. What a cycle of hopelessness.

Until I made the decision to do something radical for God, like going on a mission trip, I never realized just how much God loved me and wanted to provide for me. Provision doesn't always come in the form of money. The truth is, money doesn't make us happy—not for long, anyway. I had to let go of my own idea of what my life looked like and embrace the grace God had for me. That scared me! I didn't want to go in that direction, even though I didn't know what that direction was. I now agree with Paul, who says, "*For I can do everything through Christ, who gives me strength*" (Phil 4:13). Until I step on the grace He provides and follow my shepherd, I cannot do "all things."

We have a choice. Grace is always there. It's the path God has chosen for us. When we chose to walk on grace, regardless of the circumstances, we're lifted up over those very circumstances that want to cause us to curl up in a ball, hide, or quit before we finish. Choose grace. Ask God to show you the road of grace. It's not a well-travelled path, because it's one only you and Holy Spirit walk on side by side. He leads you, and sometimes He gives you just a little push so you don't stray off the path and fall in the ditch. Oh, the wonders of God and the glorious road He has for us! May we never lose our wonder at or sight of grace.

GOING DEEPER

REFLECTION

1. How have you witnessed God's grace in the lives of others?

2. Where have you experienced God's grace in your own life?

3. Grace is accessed as we take a step forward. In what areas do you know you need to step out so you can experience God's grace in a new way?

DECREE

So let us come boldly to the throne of our gracious God. There we will receive his mercy, and we will find grace to help us when we need it most. (Hebrews 4:16) You may think that the situation is hopeless, but God gives us more grace when we turn away from our own interests. That's why Scripture says, God opposes the proud, but He pours out grace on the humble. (James 4:6, VOICE) Sin is no longer your master, for you no longer live under the requirements of the law. Instead, you live under the freedom of God's grace. (Romans 6:14) And since it is through God's kindness, then it is not by their good works. For in that case, God's grace would not be what it really is—free and undeserved. (Romans 11:6)

PRAYER

Holy Spirit, help me to understand how grace and faith work together. Teach me how to operate by Your grace so I can do things that are impossible without You. I want to leave my independence behind and pick up grace and lean on You ... be dependent on You to help me navigate through the life I have been given. It may not look like I thought it would, but with Your help, I can enjoy my life day by day. The future You have for me will unfold in wonderful ways I never thought possible. You have given me choices where it seemed there were none. Thank you for the cross and giving Your life, Jesus, so I am no longer bound by sin. Amen.

FURTHER READING

Romans 6–8 (The Message says it best)

Grace Awakening by Charles R. Swindoll, W. Publishing Group, a division of Thomas Nelson Inc., 1990, 1996, 2003

CHAPTER NINE

FINANCES GET IN THE WAY

I was back home from the mission trip and ready for another step in my recovery. Diane had referred me to an optometrist in London, skilled in the ways of neurological optical assessments. Off I went to have my eyes checked. She told me my right eye was in a fight or flight mode, which didn't sound all that promising to me. But I was looking for answers, so this was good news—they had found something wrong. This examination also revealed that my visual centre was off. She explained the effect this had on my balance and the way I "saw" things, and prescribed bifocal prism glasses. She also suggested I sign up for some visual sessions to learn some helpful exercises.

About this time, my insurance company decided they wanted nothing more to do with me. They denied every treatment plan Diane put through for me. I went ahead and got the glasses the optometrist suggested, and for the first time in thirty years was wearing eye glasses instead of contact lenses. With bifocals and the prisms in my lens, I couldn't see unless I held my head straight and centred. My head still felt dizzy when I turned to the left or the right. It didn't take long for problems to begin to surface. I was nauseated most the time, and it was so bad my doctor prescribed nausea pills that are given to pregnant women for acute morning sickness. They didn't work at all, so I threw them out.

That month I spent most of my time lying in my adjustable bed. I held my head very still so the nausea would go away, and while it did get a little better, I felt completely off balance. I could barely function if there was a lot of movement, and my eyes became super sensitive to the light. In the dark, I couldn't function at all because I lost my sense of where I was in space. All of this would be really fascinating ... if only it wasn't happening to me.

I couldn't afford to attend the visual classes, so I shelved them for a while. My income replacement benefits had run their course, so I had no income. It was a very trying time. We had our mortgage payment, and two cars sat in the driveway.

Thinking back, I'm not sure how we managed to keep a hold on everything. I remember Dave was really busy at work—he worked six days a week with lots of overtime so we could make ends meet. Money was tight, and we learned how to budget very quickly. We always had what we needed during that time, but there wasn't any extra. We were thankful we could keep what we had, but were prepared to sell our house if necessary.

The added pressure of financial difficulties brought both Dave and I to a place of trusting in the Lord to provide what we needed. I spent twenty-six dollars one week for groceries, and we had enough to eat all week. We received money in the mail just in time for payments. A letter from our extended health insurer said we'd forgotten to cash a cheque from a year prior, so they sent us a new one. Financial miracles took place. They may seem small to some, but we were in a preparation period for what God wanted to do in our finances. We were thankful to be able to meet our financial responsibilities during this time. About three months after we started the ordeal, Dave got a large raise at work, and he ended up making enough that I didn't need to think about working. God was proving Himself to us again. We could pay all of our bills and even save some money. Things were looking better every day.

Soon the scheduled time for me to go to an "Examination of Discovery" approached. This is an official event that my lawyer and I and the lawyer from the third-party insurance company had to attend. The lawyer from the third-party insurance company asked questions upon questions, which I thought had absolutely nothing to do with my injury. I found out that they had hired a private detective to follow me around for three days. That was funny, because all they filmed me doing was walking down the street and kneeling down to tie my running shoe one day. The rest of the days I was inside.

I know this was something that had to be done, but I couldn't help feeling like I was on trial. I didn't do anything wrong, but because I had a third-party lawsuit, they had to rule out that I was faking my injury. I wasn't faking it. I wanted nothing more than to be back to where I was before the accident so I could earn my own money. The deep depression may have been gone, but self-pity was hanging on like a wet blanket. I hadn't completely come to grips with the fact that things were not going to be as they were. I was on a new journey into uncharted territory.

My lawyer told me the whole process could take up to five years before everything was settled, then I would be done with the insurance companies, assessments, doctors, and therapists. I was a little disappointed that it would take so long, but that was the way the game was played.

After being on "trial," I continued doing what I knew to do—the usual everyday things that seemed so mundane. In the big picture, it was these mundane things that got me to where I am today. Appointments were fewer and fewer. I was going to the pool twice a week, walking, exercising, and stretching at home. I was seeing Diane to receive more instruction for opening up my back, although I didn't enjoy those appointments much. I'd feel so nauseated on the way to her new office located on the other side of the city that I wanted to throw up by the time I got there.

Part of my regular routine had been walking outside, and as it got colder, I tried using a treadmill so my muscles wouldn't seize up. The treadmill was no friend. Nauseated and dizzy, I'd persevere for about five minutes then go to sit with my head in my hands. Something was out of sync for sure. I wasn't getting any better, although I was holding steady.

Good news came at Christmas time. My lawyer called and told me negotiations were beginning and a settlement was just around the corner. I'm glad I wasn't called to be a lawyer. My lawyer was a whirlwind of action—considering, computing, and concluding what would be in my best interest. I'm so thankful I had such a great person to represent me. Looking back, this was another way God looked out for me. My lawyer made everything as painless as possible, and considering I dealt with a lot of physical pain every day, I was glad I didn't have to worry about that area at all. God had everything under control, and I chose to snuggle in under His wing, trusting Him for protection by having faith that my lawyer knew what he was doing.

In the new year, I received remuneration agreed upon by both parties. It was considered a reasonable amount for the death of my former life so I could continue the new life set before me. It wasn't what I wanted, but God provided me with what I needed, as He always has throughout this journey. It certainly changed the way I looked at my recovery; I was now the one leading the charge. I could decide what I needed and go ahead without waiting for reports to be written and approvals to be signed.

In the spring, we decided it would be best to pay off our mortgage to relieve the pressure I felt to return to some sort of employment. This is a testimony to a miracle. We'd purchased our house later in our lives and had re-mortgaged twice since buying it. We were not going to be done paying for our house until well into our retirement age. In the end, we had a mortgage for eleven years. It was ironic that the previous summer we were in training to be able to handle a large sum of money, using it for the best purposes. It proved to be valuable training, as we didn't rush into what we felt we needed to do. We took our time to decide the best course of action.

When I called the mortgage company, they told me the best way to apply the money for our benefit. Who does that? Why would they care? But they did, and we took their advice—after all, they were the experts. When you can admit to yourself that you don't know everything, and that your way may not be the best way, you open yourself for God. He can then step in and guide you.

I had also been decreeing for a couple years that I was going to have a hot tub after everything was said and done. Diane had put through a treatment plan for one, but, alas, it didn't get on the approved list. I wasn't surprised. With the funds now available to do so, I got a hot tub. At this point, I gave up my wonderful massage therapist in exchange for the daily heat of the jets massaging my overworked muscles. It felt like Heaven on Earth sliding into the heat and just sitting there, feeling better by the minute. My love for my hot tub has not grown cold.

TRUST

Trust:
1. assured reliance on the character, ability, strength, or truth of someone or something;
2. one in which confidence is placed.

I never thought much of being without. I always had the means to do what had to be done in order to acquire what I needed, when I needed it. I considered myself self-sufficient all my life. I didn't have respect for money, or ultimately for the One providing me with money. I didn't consider where I worked, or that work was a privilege, until I didn't have the capability to earn money. It was a humbling experience to face the reality that I was actually relying on God to provide for me. I had always relied on my employer, or expected Dave to do what had to be done to provide what we needed. I made limitless discoveries about trusting God as my provider. He doesn't just provide the "spiritual" things in life and leave the rest up to me. He provides everything I need, and He wants to prove to me that He is faithful. When I trust and have faith that He will provide, and not lean on my own understanding, I will see that He is doing exactly what He promises in His Word.

The Bible says the love of money is the root of all kinds of evil (1 Timothy 6:10), but it doesn't say we aren't to have any. Money is the currency of the earth, and since I'm stationed here while waiting for my discharge papers so I can go home to Heaven, I want to have some of this world's money to do what I was made to do—advance the Kingdom of God on earth.

Trust flows with contentment. When I am content in who I am, I will be content with what I have, because God says His children will not have to beg for bread and that He will not forsake me, even if my mother and father forsake me (Psalm 37:25, 27:10). That's a pretty big promise! He also says not to worry about tomorrow and what you will wear or what you will eat, because if He cares for the sparrow, how much more will He take care of you ... His child (Matthew 6:25–34)?

Our problem is that we don't believe God cares enough about us to provide for us, but the truth is that God knows our heart's desires. When you suddenly get a gift you really wanted but never thought you'd have—like a hot tub—you just know you're loved and cared for. I was used to comparing my relationship with God to the relationship I had with my father—distant and cold. My father did what he knew, but he wasn't my heavenly Father who knew me before I was in my mother's womb. My earthly father provided financially, so I didn't struggle too much with letting my Father in Heaven help with financial provision. My big issue was believing that He cared. It was in this area that I thought I had to be self-sufficient and do everything myself. I couldn't trust anyone to do anything for me; I had to do it to make sure it was done right.

As I discover more of the character of God, and read His Word, He shows me in the Bible that I can trust Him. The more I trust Him, the more content I am that He knows me, sees me, cares about me, protects me, and provides for me when I let Him. Through this wonderful cycle, I'm learning to trust Him more and more. Sometimes it's more difficult to keep a "hands off" approach than it is to run ahead of God and do your own thing. For me, running ahead usually ends in a mess, leaving me to try and clean up something that never should have been there in the first place. Yes, it takes practice and time to build a relationship. Perhaps it's time to start going a little deeper with your Father in Heaven. It's a glorious thing knowing there is always more to learn about Him, and each step of the way your trust in Him grows. Ask God to help you trust Him. Tell Him where you want to trust Him more so you can have more contentment. He's not far off; He's all around. He surrounds you, and He knows everything about you, so it's not going to be a surprise to Him.

GOING DEEPER

REFLECTION

1. What do you think of when you hear the word *trust*?

2. In what areas is it easy for you to trust God? In what area is it difficult?

3. Why is it difficult to trust Him in those areas?

4. Take some time and let Holy Spirit into those areas where you are having a difficult time letting go. Give them to God to look after.

DECREE

Trust in the Lord with all your heart; do not depend on your own understanding. Seek his will in all you do, and he will show you which path to take. Don't be impressed with your own wisdom. Instead, fear the Lord and turn away from evil. Then you will have healing for your body and strength for your bones. Honor the Lord with your wealth and with the best part of everything you produce. Then he will fill your barns with grain, and your vats will overflow with good wine. My child, don't reject the Lord's discipline, and don't be upset when he corrects you. For the Lord corrects those he loves, just as a father corrects a child in whom he delights. (Proverbs 3:5–12) Give your burdens to the Lord, and he will take care of you. He will not permit the godly to slip and fall. (Psalm 55:22) The Lord is good, a strong refuge when trouble comes. He is close to those who trust in him. (Nahum 1:7) So humble yourselves under the mighty power of God, and at the right time he will lift you up in honor. Give all your worries and cares to God, for he cares about you. (1 Peter 5:6–7) Don't love money; be satisfied with what you have. For God has said, "I will never fail you. I will never abandon you." (Hebrews 13:5)

PRAYER

Jesus, I want to trust You more. I cannot do that on my own. I need Your help. I have lived my way for so long. I don't know any other way, but You are faithful and I trust You will show me the way and teach me how to depend on You and trust in You. I want to believe all the promises in Your Word; help me to believe where I have unbelief, and help me to trust that You have the best for me and will never leave me. I want to feel Your presence through Holy Spirit every day, all day long. I know this takes practice by turning my focus to You more and more as I walk along this path You have for me. Thank You for Your blood, Jesus, that cleanses and heals me every day. Amen.

FURTHER READING

Psalm 27

Matthew 6:25–34

The Blessed Life by Robert Norris, Chosen Books, 2002

Time to Prosper by Chuck Pierce, Regal from Gospel Light, 2013

CHAPTER TEN

I ONCE WAS BLIND

By summer there was no improvement on my part. My vision was quite blurry at times, and I continued to have nausea, daily headaches, and constant pain in my shoulders, head, and upper back muscles. Diane was concerned. There was more going on than what she could help me with at her office, so she recommended that I see an ophthalmologist specializing in visual therapy for people with traumatic brain injuries. There was a drawback, however—his office was a three-hour drive from where I lived. I had nothing to lose and everything to gain, so I went to be assessed once again. My insurance company hadn't accepted the first optometrist's report that something was wrong with my vision, so I wasn't counting on them to get on board with this treatment. It was one of those, "I'm doing it because it seems like something that may help," moments. What I didn't know was that this was the beginning of another difficult leg of my recovery.

I arrived at the office and was greeted by beautiful people. The doctor was exceptional and explained things thoroughly. The staff was helpful and knowledgeable. Thank goodness, because the tests were a little different than anything I'd experienced before. They placed electrodes on my head, and all I had to do was look at a screen ... strange, to say the least. After the involuntary testing, my eyes were checked in the way I was familiar with. It didn't take long before I was back in his office, waiting to hear what they'd discovered. First, I received some good news. My visual centre had re-aligned, and I didn't need the prism glasses any longer. I was going to be getting new glasses. The unfortunate part was that now I would have two pairs of glasses—a pair for distance and a pair for reading.

I was also informed that my brain injury affected my visual perception, or the way I saw things. I would need to attend visual therapy sessions to re-train my brain to see properly. The whole process would take forty weeks at minimum, with a visit to their office every other week. The therapy was very expensive and included a three-hour trip each way, so now transportation had to be considered. I was speechless, which was a feat not easily achieved. This wasn't something I could plunge into; I had to count the cost in many ways. Could I drive myself for six hours every other week? If not, who would I get to take me? I was going to need help to do some of the exercises, so my family was going to be involved as well. I needed to ask for help. I thought of it as losing more of myself and my life instead of what it really was—losing control. With lots of questions and lots of doubts, I faced a crossroad again.

I went home to discuss the treatment with my support team. This was a big decision. I desperately wanted to get better. It had been three-and-a-half years since my car accident. Was there much sense in doing this now? Wasn't it too late? Pastor C. assured me it would benefit me spiritually, physically, and emotionally. Diane assured me that it wasn't too late, I wasn't too old, and I could do this. My family was all for it and more than willing to help in any way they could. I decided to go for it without having all the details, which was probably a good thing. All I knew at the beginning was I'd be doing eye exercises and going on a six-hour drive every other week. I talked to some friends, and it was loosely agreed that someone would be available to get me to my appointments if I couldn't drive myself. So off I went on another adventure.

I was torn between the excitement of entering into something that would push me into what I thought would be the fullness of recovery, and the fear of what I'd have to do to get there. I had put great expectation on the outcome of this treatment. This was it. I was nearing the end of this prison sentence. I had a positive attitude, but I lacked correct perception. I guess that's why I was going to brain-retraining sessions disguised as visual therapy. I needed my brain retrained and my mind renewed. In the fall, I started the process of having my whole perception of the world around me changed.

It turned out that I could go by myself, and those long drives all alone ended up being very intimate times with God. I was learning how much He loved me and that He didn't want to leave me the way I was. In fact, in His eyes I was already healed, I just had to walk the path He had laid out in front of me—the path to wholeness. It was going to be work, and once again I learned how very strong I am when I allow God to walk with me and show me the plans He has for me.

After the first therapy session, I knew exactly what was expected of me. I had about five different exercises to do every day that took about twenty minutes. I needed help with some, but others I could do alone. I had to chart everything, including my reaction to the exercises. I discovered that the exercises I needed help with were the hardest and most frustrating. All of the exercises brought on symptoms that made me feel sick. It was horrible! My head and neck hurt, my stomach rolled, I could actually feel my brain hurting, and I was angry. Obviously, I didn't want to do them, but I had paid in advance for half the treatment. It was expensive, and I wasn't going to quit.

After a couple of months, the exercises got easier. I wasn't quite so angry at those who loved me and were only trying to help me succeed. The symptoms were either lessening in intensity, or I was getting used to them.

They tested me to assess my progress, and things were moving along right on schedule. I enjoy playing video games, and one would think I'd be excited when they added a daily regime of computer-generated exercises ... after all, I got to wear 3-D glasses! My visual technician didn't give me these exercises/games right away so as to accustom me (I guess) to the feelings of nausea and physical pain before the addition of intense eye pain. This was no kid's game. These games were not fun, and they brought on very real, intense eye pain. I referred to them as "The Eye Invasion Games."

During this season, I was continuing the devotional I'd started on the eternal perspective of circumstances, and God was changing the way I thought. He was teaching me how to see the world around me from His perspective. I started to understand that I could be in any circumstance and He would show me what He saw in each situation. His ways are not our ways; His thoughts are not our thoughts (Isaiah 58:8). This became very obvious to me in the year to come.

RENEWING YOUR MIND

Retrain:

1. to teach (someone) new skills: to train (someone) again;
2. to learn new skills, especially for a different job;
3. to train again or anew.

Renew: to make something new, fresh, or strong again.

Blessings open doors of blessing. Cursing opens doors of curses. We reap what we sow, which is why it's so important to renew our minds. God wants us to know who we are through His eyes so we won't be cursing ourselves by saying that we aren't who He clearly says we are.

The battle is in our mind. We may not be able to change our outward circumstances, but with Holy Spirit and God's Word, we can change how we think. When we change what we're thinking about, we'll learn to change what we're saying about ourselves and others. What we think, we believe—and what we believe in our heart, we say (Matthew 12:3).

Changing the way we think actually changes how we see what's in front of us. When we see through a positive lens, we have faith to believe that the expected end will be for our good. A negative lens always causes us to see our circumstances as something to get through, without a vision for the end; in fact, we keep thinking there is no end. This was my problem! My injury existed in my visual centre. My brain perceived incorrectly when I looked through my eyes. Although I had totally submitted to the process of renewing my vision, I had a bad attitude concerning some of my treatment. It's realistic to be fearful when you start something unknown, but when you allow fear to take over, the negative will emerge. By submitting that fear to God and asking Holy Spirit to help, things will move into the proper perspective, and you can continue the process.

Renewing our thought processes and how we think about life actually has two sides—our mind and our brain. When learning new ways of doing things (or re-training our brains after a trauma occurs), we need to go back to the beginning and start over in some areas. That's what they did at vision therapy. The exercises I did at the beginning actually removed some things I had previously known, and the new exercises put back what I had lost. I had to get back to the starting point before I could move forward and be made whole. Isn't that what we do when we have wrong beliefs and mindsets? The Lord wants to take us back to the beginning, to our first love, Jesus, and then start building our foundation on truth. I was retraining my brain to see correctly, both spiritually and naturally.

The renewing part happens to your mind by renewing your thoughts. As a result, your actions come from focusing on a particular pattern of thinking. First, Holy Spirit helps you realize that your thought process isn't in alignment with the truth, and then you apply what He says to renew that old pattern of thinking. Sometimes it happens quickly, and sometimes it takes further examining of ourselves and why we think that way. Our mindsets determine how we filter what we hear. If our patterns of thinking are not lined up with God's, and we want to move forward into that greener pasture where those boundaries keep us safe, we must push through those wrong mindsets and change them to the mind of Christ.

Patterns of thinking don't change by themselves. Even with revelation from God about that mindset, we still have our part to play. God is not magic. He wants us to partner with Him so we will feel a sense of accomplishment and, value the freedom we receive. We all enjoy that feeling of accomplishment—"Look what I did with God!" This is how our trust in Him continues to grow.

During this process, I focussed on seeing things from a different perspective. I discovered that in my heart I didn't have a positive attitude about a lot of things. I was a positive person trapped inside negative mindsets. There was only one way I could release the optimistic positive person I was made to be: I had to renew my mind and see things the way God saw them. My circumstances weren't great, but God didn't want me to remain angry and frustrated. He gave me hope in the form of vision therapy. As I pushed through and worked at it for almost a year, I accomplished far more in the spiritual atmosphere around me than I could possibly understand at that time. I knew about spiritual warfare, and that everything I did in the natural had some parallel effect on the spiritual world around me, but I couldn't see what the end would look like. Who knows what tomorrow will bring? We do what needs to get done today, because tomorrow will have its own troubles (Matthew 6:34).

In the end, contending for my change of perspective helped me to push through the tough and seemingly endless exercises that hurt my eyes and my brain. It helped to keep discouragement, and ultimately depression, at bay so that my heart could continue to heal. I was walking on grace, and if I stepped off that path, it didn't take long for me to see I needed Holy Spirit to help me. I couldn't do this alone, and some days I felt defeated.

I called friends, got prayer, and learned that family and community had a big role to play in my recovery. God made us to work together and be interdependent on each other. Without people to encourage and cheer me on, I wouldn't have completed this difficult but necessary segment of my walk.

As we move forward and keep in the cycle of renewing our mind and retraining our brain, we can start to tell our brain to line up with what God says about us, and we can actually tell our bodies through our brain to line up and get into the proper position.

GOING DEEPER

REFLECTION

1. What is my outlook on life?

2. What comes out of our mouths is a reflection of what's in our hearts and minds. Listen to what is coming out of your mouth. What are you saying about yourself and your situations?

3. Practice aligning your thoughts and speech to what God says about you by capturing your thoughts and plugging in the truth. What thoughts do you wrestle with the most?

DECREE

Guard your heart above all else, for it determines the course of your life. (Proverbs 4:23) Don't copy the behaviour and customs of this world, but let God transform you into a new person by changing the way you think. Then you will learn to know God's will for you, which is good and pleasing and perfect. (Romans 12:2) And you will know the truth, and the truth will set you free. (John 8:32) And now, dear brothers and sisters, one final thing. Fix your thoughts on what is true, and honorable, and right, and pure, and lovely, and admirable. Think about things that are excellent and worthy of praise. (Philippians 4:8) For, "Who can know the LORD's thoughts? Who knows enough to teach him?" But we understand these things, for we have the mind of Christ. (1 Corinthians 2:16)

PRAYER

Father, I know I have wrong mindsets that need to be lined up with what You say about me. Please help me to get into the cycle of renewing my mind with Your Word and changing those old patterns of wrong thinking into God-thinking. I am willing to do my part in this process, and where I'm unwilling, help me to be willing. Help me to capture negative thoughts and replace them with God thoughts—what You say about me in Your Word. I want to think the thoughts of Heaven here on earth. I want to be all You have created me to be. Help me to see myself from Your perspective. In Jesus' name. Amen.

FURTHER READING

Psalm 51 (VOICE)

The Battlefield of the Mind by Joyce Meyer, Life in the Word Inc., 1995

CHAPTER ELEVEN

THE JAW

It was now almost four years since my accident, and I had adjusted to my new lifestyle. It wasn't what I preferred, but I was managing well and learning to live with daily pain. I continued to wake up with headaches, but taking a couple of pills and resting for an hour or so kept the pain manageable. If I behaved myself that day, I could enjoy tomorrow; if not, I paid the consequences with more pain.

In what seemed like overnight, I started to experience extreme jaw pain. The left side of my jaw sometimes ached, but this intense pain ran across my upper jaw, radiating down into my lower jaw. I sat for hours with heat on my face, as it seemed to be the only thing that brought relief. I knew a visit with Diane was in order. It just so happened that she had recently been to a pain seminar and sat next to a dentist, of all people. She said they had discussed jaw injury caused by trauma and asked me if I would be interested in going to see him about my jaw. Talk about divine appointments and being in the right place at the right time! Before I had time to think about it, I had an appointment with a dentist specializing in temporomandibular joint (TMJ) and sleep disorders.

While waiting for my appointment, I had a lot of down time applying heat and trying different techniques to control the pain. There is nothing like head pain. It must be because it's so close to your brain that it hurts so bad. While I was doing a lot of lying and sitting around, disappointment and discouragement were right there, hoping to get a foothold in me. I was certainly disappointed. What was going on? I was doing what I was supposed to do, and now this was happening. Self-pity was threatening to get a good grip on me. Luckily, I didn't have too long to wait to see what was going on, and I decided to keep a positive attitude.

I had worked for a dentist, and now I was going to see one. Again, I met wonderful people who love what they do, and it certainly showed. I was once again undergoing tests I'd never heard of or seen before. This wasn't an ordinary dentist. I expected to have to wait for the results, but they surprised me. I was given a temporary, gel-filled gadget that I put in my mouth, and in about ten minutes, the pain was gone and relief flooded throughout my body. I was going to be alright. Something helped—even if it was only temporary. It was enough until I knew what was going on.

Because Diane had referred me there, they were going to put through a treatment plan to see if my insurance company would foot the bill. I wanted to go ahead with the treatment immediately, as the effects had been so positive. I had no pain in my jaw at all, and it actually relieved some of the pain in the back of my head as well. I knew this was only temporary and I'd need more treatment. This was a major disappointment. I had thought the visual therapy was the end of this journey to wholeness. I couldn't release the disappointment, so discouragement came on strongly.

No one looking from the outside (unless I decided to be completely honest) knew how discouraged I was. I'd been very good at hiding the deadly D's (see Chapter 4) during this whole ordeal, so most of my church family, friends, and some family members didn't know how much pain I lived in and how much I hurt inside because of the dramatic change in my lifestyle. I was learning a lot about how to deal with myself and allowing God to heal me instead of just coping. There were those who shared the burden with me—my husband, my pastor, my daughters who lived with us, my son and daughter-in-law, a couple of close friends, and my sister.

This time was tough. When you've put all your eggs in one basket and it doesn't pan out, it hurts a lot when the basket falls. Self-pity moved in and set up camp at my house. I didn't outwardly show it much, but it constantly spoke to me, telling me just how bad it was. As I started to go back into that familiar pit, I realized what was going on and refused to slip down into that black hole. I knew that if I didn't choose to fight and stand firm, I'd slide down the slick walls of that hole and it would be a hard climb out. I saw a movie once in which a woman running in a downpour of rain fell into a deep hole that was eventually going to be an in-ground pool. She slid right to the bottom, and the walls were so high and slippery, she couldn't get out. While she was in that hole, which was filling up with muddy water, a bunch of dead things started floating by—a very fearful place to be. Eventually, someone threw a rope down to her. That was the only way out, so of course she took it—you'd be a fool not to take the way out.

This image comes to mind now because it describes exactly what depression felt like to me. I wasn't going back there, but I had to choose to stand and fight in order to win the battle; otherwise, the dead things of my past would drown me. God was teaching me that it's okay to request help. I didn't have to fight those battles alone. He had provided a way out, and I just had to ask for help. Would I be a fool, or would I humble myself and tell someone what was going on? Something supernatural happens when you share the dark secrets of your heart. Confessing them out loud releases the hold they have on you, and that's exactly what happened. The pit disappeared from sight, and in its place hope returned ... and I could breathe again.

EXPECTATIONS

Expectation:

1. a belief that something will happen or is likely to happen;
2. a feeling or belief about how successful, good, etc., someone or something will be.

When your expectations don't come to pass, what a mess it can create! I thank God that He loves coming into our messes. After all, His son, Jesus, was born in a messy stable; messes don't intimidate Him at all. Now that I'm on the other side of those few years of my life, I'm amazed and in awe of how God carried me through. I was in the last stretch of vision therapy, and I felt like I was blindsided and knocked down for the count. I didn't even think of stopping at this point; I could hardly think at all, because I was in so much pain.

Disappointment from unmet expectations is deadly and needs to be dealt with quickly before it turns into self-pity or a feeling of melancholy, both of which are forms of depression. They taunt you with voices of defeat that don't stop on their own. You must replace those thoughts with good ones ... thoughts that produce the strength to continue onward.

When we place our expectations in the Lord, He will renew our strength and heal our hurting hearts. I learned that when those negative voices began, I first had to recognize that they weren't my thoughts. They were the voice of satan, the enemy of my soul, speaking thoughts and ideas into my mind. Once I recognized that they weren't mine, I captured them by simply saying, "No, that's a lie." I'd find a key scripture or two to help for that period of time and spoke, wrote, and meditated on them until they were what remained in my mind. I was creating a habit of positive thinking. This wasn't easy, because I'd been hearing those voices all my life, not just since my accident. But because I'd been renewing my mind with the Word of God, I could recognize that what I was hearing was not truth. I now had a choice: I could replace those lying words with truth, or let them run freely through my mind.

When I chose to replace negative thoughts with positive ones, I had the strength to face my wrong expectations. God could heal my heart, and I could begin to place my expectations in Him. I still believed I could be healed and whole, but I continued forward with the end in mind. My main focus shifted to where it should be ... to God and my relationship with Him.

Be encouraged. It takes practice. We all make mistakes when we start something new. When we think of those set backs as failure because we expected a different end, we must get up and say, "No." We always learn something when we fail, and if we can take what we learned and apply it to our lives, it's not failure at all. It's called learning from our mistakes. As we take what we learned and focus on God, He will lead us far beyond any expectations we could ever imagine and into wide open spaces of His love!

GOING DEEPER

REFLECTION

1. Ask Holy Spirit to help you identify some thoughts you have right now that are not from Him. Record what He shows you.

2. Declare that those are not your thoughts.

3. Find a couple of scriptures that state the truth about that thought according to God and begin declaring it over yourself. This begins to create the habit of positive thinking based on your identity in Christ.

4. What would you say is your focus? Ask Holy Spirit to help you shift it off the end result and onto Him.

DECREE

God means what he says. What he says goes. His powerful Word is sharp as a surgeon's scalpel, cutting through everything, whether doubt or defense, laying us open to listen and obey. Nothing and no one is impervious to God's Word. We can't get away from it—no matter what. (Hebrews 4:12–13, MSG) But those who trust in the Lord will find new strength. They will soar high on wings like eagles. They will run and not grow weary. They will walk and not faint. (Isaiah 40:31) God, the one and only—I'll wait as long as he says. Everything I hope for comes from him, so why not? He's solid rock under my feet, breathing room for my soul, an impregnable castle: I'm set for life. My help and glory are in God —granite-strength and safe-harbor-God—So trust him absolutely, people; lay your lives on the line for Him. God is a safe place to be. (Psalm 62:5–7, MSG)

PRAYER

Father, I thank You for all you have done for me. I'm grateful for the past victories, and as we work together, I know You're working out the best You have for me. I want my expectation to be firmly in You. You knew me before I was even formed; You know me better than I know myself. You know my deepest heart's desires, and You know what's best for me, because You love me so much. Help me to trust You. Help me to believe the promises of Your words to me that are written in the Bible. In my weakness You are strong, and I need Your strength to carry me through this season. In Jesus' name I pray. Amen.

FURTHER READING

Psalm 27

2 Timothy 3:16–17

From There to Here

Psalm 142

Power Thoughts by Joyce Meyer, Faith Works, 2010

CHAPTER TWELVE

THE JAW TWO

A couple of weeks after my initial examination, I went back to the dentist to find out that he could help me. The X-rays showed that my jaw was out of position. I was progressing in retraining my brain through visual therapy, but my jaw couldn't align properly without treatment. I'd need to wear an appliance all day and a different one at night for three to four months to realign my jaw. He told me that I'd need to wear the night appliance for the rest of my life. On paper that doesn't sound too bad, considering what I'd been through up to this point, but my experience working with a dentist for twenty years told me that this was going to be a difficult, narrow road to walk on—or chew on, in my case.

I went home to count the cost, came back, and agreed to the treatment. In a short time, I was sent home with custom-made appliances. I had to follow a healing diet while I wore the day appliance for a three-month period. The foods allowed were limited—caffeine free tea, fish, eggs, vegetables, fruit, and butter. Prohibited foods included sugar, yeast, and dairy. The appliance that sat on top of my bottom teeth made chewing difficult, so I was to eat cooked food only. This made for a very interesting three months.

I continued with vision therapy and discovered that some of the exercises were very easy now that my jaw was in alignment. My balance was restored, and I believe it's probably better now than it had been for most of my life. However, symptoms started emerging, and I was starting to feel overwhelmed and over-stimulated in everyday tasks. My brain was on overload and couldn't process all that was going on. The jaw affects your whole body, and mine was now moving in the right position. I had more pain in my head, shoulders, and upper back as everything shifted to a new position.

Shortly after the pain began, I knew from previous experience that this wasn't necessarily a bad thing. My body was adjusting, but what threw me off was the overwhelming feeling I experienced in the everyday things that had never been a problem before. Diane assured me that I wasn't going crazy, but suggested that I might have to back off on some of the treatment for a little while to give my brain time to catch up. I couldn't stop the jaw treatment, so vision therapy was put on hold. This was another disappointment, but I hadn't suffered previously in vain. I had learned to choose to be positive. I believe that taking that path right away was the final push in removing self-pity from my life. I exploded forward in my recovery, both physically and spiritually.

I only missed two appointments for vision therapy and continued to do a couple of daily essential exercises to maintain what I'd gained up to that point. I stuck to the healing diet without even batting an eye at the coffee and chocolate I couldn't have. I also went to my final insurance assessment during this time. God is funny. The last assessment I ever had was with a dentist, and I smile every time I think of that moment. A dentist's office was the one place I could go where I felt confident, because that was a world I knew.

After examining me and seeing my X-rays, the dentist couldn't deny the before and after. I felt such peace, because finally I didn't have to prove to anyone that something was wrong with me. God knew there was something wrong, and He loved me so much that He opened doors for me to get the best treatment and access to the best professionals. I didn't receive a copy of the assessment report, because shortly after this appointment, my case with my insurance company was settled and my file was stamped closed. Over three years, I accumulated two boxes of reports and letters from insurance adjusters, lawyers, medical doctors, dentists, physical therapists, chiropractors, assessors, professors, psychologists, psychiatrists, optometrists, and ophthalmologists that measure over two feet high. Those pages represent a lot of emotions I had to deal with up close and personal—emotions that didn't fit in the happy and angry boxes I started with at the beginning of my journey. I had acquired an integral skill of considering and evaluating my emotions so I could understand what I was really feeling.

I was going to keep those reports the required time and then burn them. Now I think I'll keep them in a pile somewhere where I can walk by them, glance at them like a memorial stone, and remember that the Lord has done great things for me and in me. What a wild ride, and it wasn't over yet! Exciting times were ahead. The next phase of treatment was literally all in my head.

POSITIVE CONFESSION

> Alignment: the proper positioning or state of adjustment of parts in relation to each other.

> Confession: (yadah) to throw, to shoot (arrows), to cast, throw down; to give thanks, laud, praise. (www.blueletterbible.org/lang/Lexicon/Lexicon.cfm?strongs=H3034&t=KJV)

When I first started following Jesus, I thought a lot about what was written in the Bible. I loved reading it, and I always found just the right words to help me get through the situations I faced. I've never been very good at remembering where the verses were found, but I remembered the words, and that's okay. The original transcripts of the Bible didn't have chapters and verses attached to them anyway.

I've had the best teachers, and I'm grateful they stressed to me to not only read the Word, but to speak it out loud into the atmosphere. It's great to know the Word of God, but it doesn't accomplish what it was meant to until you begin to declare it. It stays as head knowledge. Lasting change can only occur from the inside out. When you declare the Word and then hear it, it can't help but change you, because it is a living Word. Since faith comes by hearing the Word of God, and we need faith to believe, we must speak the Word out loud for ourselves. It builds our faith for those things we hope for that we cannot see yet, both for our loved ones and ourselves. I've learned that the amount of declaring the Word you do determines the level of freedom you can achieve and maintain.

When my jaw was placed in the right position and my body started to re-adjust into alignment, it was painful and my brain couldn't adjust fast enough, probably because it was still in recovery mode. God will take us to our limits and beyond to stretch us so we can grow and mature.

Alignment is interesting. My jaw was placed in the proper position—where it hadn't been for a long time; it was slightly out of alignment before the accident. God wants to put our jaws/mouths in alignment with what He says about us so He can speak through us. We are His ambassadors on earth. We represent Him, and if we're not confessing what He says about us, how do we ever expect to believe it? Belief comes from hearing the Word, which we can then obey, affecting those in our world. That's how we become agents of change. When we're judgemental, critical, and say things that aren't in alignment with God's Word, we remain a negative person and our mind stays un-renewed.

Words are so important. God created the heavens and the earth with His Word, and when we are in alignment with Him, we will hear what He is saying and can join with Him to change our world with our words. That is the power Jesus died on the cross to give us—the power to experience blind eyes seeing, deaf ears hearing, the mute speaking, the lame walking, and sickness being healed. What an awesome responsibility— one we often take far too casually.

Words build up or tear down. Sometimes we want to tear down wrong mindsets and wrong beliefs, but not at the cost of tearing down other people's character. Relationship is very important to God—far more important than being right. When we ask for and work towards a change in perspective, we'll also be able to respond in loving ways with our mouths.

The Bible says that no one can tame the tongue, and that it's restless and evil, full of deadly poison (James 3:8). When we engage in the process of becoming whole, we must ask God to help us use self-control over our mouths and bind our mouths to what Holy Spirit would have us say. I didn't realize just how much the jaw affects the rest of our body until I went through this experience. My balance was restored almost instantly and, like it or not, my whole body moved to adjust to the new position of my jaw. It's fascinating how we are made and how everything in our body connects together.

When I used to think of the word "confess," I'd experience feelings of guilt, because if I was confessing something, it usually meant that I'd done something wrong. Sometimes that's the case, but according to *Strong's Concordance*, the original meaning of the word is "yadah," which is a praise word, or a word for giving thanks. I had twisted many things in my mind that God wanted to unravel so that He could show me His thoughts—the truth of the matter.

Confessing, decreeing, and declaring truth is giving thanks and praising God, which is another way we can worship God through our words. God wants us to speak out who we are, who He is, and His Word concerning matters that are important to the forward movement of the Kingdom. That's how we move those mountains in front of us. The more we use our voices for good and not evil, the more we will change, because we can only consistently say what we believe in our hearts. The more we say the truth, the more we will believe it. A truly beautiful cycle. Once we let God in to change us, our talk will change and our walk will become more balanced. Food for thought—the Kingdom of God is voice-activated.

GOING DEEPER

REFLECTION

1. What kinds of things (positive or negative) are you currently confessing about yourself?

2. In what ways do you want to change your confession?

3. Write out what the Bible says about you. Ask Holy Spirit to show you where you are not believing this truth. Choose one and begin to confess the truth about who you are over yourself.

DECREE

Today I have given you the choice between life and death, between blessings and curses. Now I call on heaven and earth to witness the choice you make. Oh, that you would choose life, so that you and your descendants might live! (Deuteronomy 30:19) So faith comes from hearing, that is, hearing the Good News about Christ. (Romans 10:17) I said to myself, "I will watch what I do and not sin in what I say. I will hold my tongue when the ungodly are around me." (Psalm 39:1) Words satisfy the mind as much as fruit does the stomach; good talk is as gratifying as a good harvest. Words kill, words give life; they're either poison or fruit—you choose. (Proverbs 18:20–21, MSG) Let my tongue sing about your word, for all your commands are right. (Psalm 119:172).

PRAYER

Father, I desire that the words of my mouth be pleasing to You. I repent of using my tongue as a weapon to tear down instead of building up and encouraging people. I repent of using my mouth to speak negatively about myself. Cleanse my heart and help me through the power of Holy Spirit, who lives in me, to change my ways and change my words to be filled with life and love. Align my jaw so I can live a balanced life and further the Kingdom of God by my voice. I choose blessing over curses, and am determined to speak life to everyone in my world, including myself. In Jesus' name I pray. Amen.

FURTHER READING

James 3:1–12

Psalm 101

Girls with Swords by Lisa Bevere, Waterbrook Press, 2013

The Bait of Satan by John Bevere, Charisma House, 2004

CHAPTER THIRTEEN

OUT WITH THE OLD

I was progressing well with my jaw treatment. After wearing the day appliance for approximately three-months, I left it at the dentist's office, walking a new and much more balanced walk. He suggested seeing a craniosacral therapist to help adjust my head with my jaw. I didn't know anything about craniosacral therapy, and I couldn't even say the word until about three months into treatment! My mouth felt different, and my teeth didn't come together quite the same. Things had definitely changed, and I had jaw pain again. Not the same pain as previously, mind you—this felt more like a healing pain, similar to when you are in recovery on the way to wholeness.

I agreed to see the recommended craniosacral therapist. I found this to be the most fascinating thing I've ever experienced. Vision therapy (which is really brain re-training), having my jaw re-aligned, and learning how both affected my body were amazing experiences, but this was entirely different.

Each session lasted an hour. When Joy, my craniosacral therapist, first assessed me, she explained the process knowledgably and in terms I could understand. I didn't realize that our head has twenty-three bones; I naively thought that our skull was all one bone that fused together when we were young children. I learned that our entire body, including our head, was surrounded by a membrane called fascia.

At the first appointment, I lay there and felt nothing. She had such a light touch, and I was very skeptical. I was used to the much more vigorous work of the chiropractor. It seemed to me she was just holding my head and feeling my feet ... and then she sent me home. When I got home, I was very tired. The next day, I felt like a truck had hit me—aches and pains all over, and I could feel that something had shifted. It seemed small, but I knew something was happening, and I didn't particularly like it. She'd told me I'd feel like this, but I didn't believe her.

After that first appointment, I knew deep inside that this was going to work for me, even though I didn't like the after-effects of those first few appointments. Whenever I was there I'd ask questions and listen very closely to her answers; not only did my bones get treatment, but I learned important strategies that have helped me get my brain on board quickly. After the initial residual effects wore off, I became more aware and was able to feel what she was doing and how it affected my body. I was pleased with my progress, and I was feeling better. I still had headaches, but not every day and not as intense. I could do more in a day, and I liked being more productive.

During this time, the company my husband worked for went bankrupt. He needed to find a new job, and almost had a new position, but it didn't work out in the end. Then something happened that neither one of us ever thought possible—an opportunity came up for him to start a business. It was sent from God. We took it and became the owners of a manufacturing company. It was a busy time, getting equipment purchased and putting financing in place, all while our customer waited for us to start production. I had a financial background, and we decided I could manage the office from home. I could spread out the work and do it throughout the day—a perfect job for me. I was excited and scared all at the same time. My re-introduction to the workforce was a gradual incline, which worked well for me. I adjusted to the changes well and thought I was moving forward.

In the natural course of the treatment, I came to a plateau and stopped progressing. This was something even Joy couldn't predict, because we're all so unique. I was stuck, and I was not happy about it. I wasn't angry, because I'd dealt with a lot of those anger issues and had learned how to release anger quickly and move on, but I was frustrated. What was happening?

Joy explained to me that we were creating new pathways in my brain, not just in my physical head. My brain was so used to the old ways (the position the bones in my head had been put in by the trauma) that it was reverting back to the old pathways or patterns. I had to change in order for my brain to allow the new pathways to remain. The bones in my head had to stay in the right position. I had to do something different in order to get different results. This was my choice, of course. What would you choose?

She advised that it would be in my best interest to cut back on physical activity. This was not the kind of news I wanted to hear. After all, I wasn't doing that much. I was able to admit that there were things I could cut back on for a short time, if it would help. I had experienced enough healing since starting treatment to know she wouldn't tell me to cut back for no reason.

I went home with my head in some sort of order to start a new segment of recovery ... rest and more rest. I didn't know what this was going to look like going forward. It seemed all

I did was sit around and lie down. I managed to keep up with the business duties, but it was hard to reduce my activities. They were pretty much essential to the running of my home. My daughters did all of the cleaning, and I made dinner and occasionally threw in a load of laundry. I sought help to carry things, and even timed the grocery shopping so someone would be home to bring the bags into the house. I knew that if I wanted to advance, I had to do what needed to be done ... which in this case was nothing physical.

It was still summer, but I couldn't content myself to enjoy any of the time relaxing. I made myself do it and felt no peace whatsoever for most of those "resting" times. The good news is that it worked. As I continued to persevere, my brain adjusted and my bones stayed where they belonged.

OLD PATTERNS, NEW PATHWAYS

Pattern:

1. a reliable sample of traits, acts, tendencies or other observable characteristics of a person, group, or institution;
2. the regular repeated way in which something happens or is done.

Most of us want release from the things that hold us in destructive patterns, or take us nowhere, but often we can become stuck or want to give up. Getting into alignment and staying there takes effort—we can't just wait for things to change. We must partner with Holy Spirit to change the way we do things in order to move forward.

I battled with my flesh constantly during this period of time. I had a new routine that was working for me. I can't say I was comfortable, because the pain was still there. It would ease off for a bit after my appointments and then return the same as always. I determined that I didn't just want relief ... I wanted to be made whole, so I had to make changes again.

As humans we are constantly moving, from the rotating Earth we live on to the people in our world, to ourselves. Nothing stays the same, yet we look for that consistency, that assurance. Jesus is the same, yesterday, today, and forever (Hebrews 8:13). He is someone we can rely on to always be there for us.

We gravitate to the old pathways—the old familiar ways we do things—when we sense change is in the air. Those well-worn methods that always seem to work suddenly don't give the results we're looking for. When that happens, we have a choice to make. Will I remain here in this old pattern, taking that familiar path, or will I take a step of faith and go where God is leading me? He will always give us the choice to let Him lead. When we choose to follow, He guides us. We may find ourselves in a position where we easily see the new path in front of us, or we may have to wait until the Shepherd reveals that path to us. When He does, we'll know it's the right one, because we'll feel inner peace—not the temporary peace that comes when our flesh is satisfied, but the peace that surpasses all our understanding. We just know that we know; it's God, and it's the right way to go.

We all have things in our lives that stop us from taking the first step on a new path. The familiar, well-worn paths lead to strongholds in our minds. Once we start confessing the positive, we'll feel the resistance of the unhealed part of our soul, because it wants its own way. It doesn't want to go into the great unknown, following the Spirit in us. Often God's path is a narrow path. Does that sound familiar? It's the narrow road as opposed to the wide one that leads to death. The road always seems narrower to me until I get going, and then it suddenly seems to grow wider as I experience more freedom walking in the new pattern of thinking.

GOING DEEPER

REFLECTION

1. What are some old patterns that are destructive to you? Ask Holy Spirit to show you.

2. What old patterns might you be ready to let go of?

3. What stops you from wanting to let go and begin a new path?

4. What is a step you can take towards change?

DECREE

So it comes down to this: since you have been raised with the Anointed One, the Liberating King, set your mind on heaven above. The Anointed is there, seated at God's right hand. Stay focused on what's above, not on earthly things, because your old life is dead and gone. Your new life is now hidden, enmeshed with the Anointed who is in God. On that day when the Anointed One—who is our very life—is revealed, you will be revealed with Him in glory! So kill your earthly impulses: loose sex, impure actions, unbridled sensuality, wicked thoughts, and greed (which is essentially idolatry). It's because of these that God's wrath is coming [upon the sons and daughters of disobedience], so avoid them at all costs. These are the same things you once pursued, and together you spawned a life of evil. But now make sure you shed such things: anger, rage, spite, slander, and abusive language. And don't go on lying to each other since you have sloughed away your old skin along with its evil practices for a fresh new you, which is continually renewed in knowledge according to the image of the One who created you. (Colossians 3:1–10, VOICE) O my soul, come, praise the Eternal; sing a song from a grateful heart; sing and never forget all the good He has done. Despite all your many offenses, He forgives and releases you. More than any doctor, He heals your diseases. He reaches deep into the pit to deliver you from death. He crowns you with unfailing love and compassion like a king. When your soul is famished and withering, He fills you with good and beautiful things, satisfying you as long as you live. He makes you strong like an eagle, restoring your youth. (Psalm 103:2–5, VOICE)

PRAYER

Jesus my Lord, help me to break out of this old pattern of thinking. I'm looking at the narrow road as something to be feared, when in reality it's what I long for, because it's one step closer to You and the destiny You have pre-ordained for me. Regardless of the trauma I have suffered, Your plan remains the same. You want to lead me down the righteous path that You have made specifically for me. It's a path where we walk together, allowing me to know You more and more. Help me to walk confidently down this new path, knowing You are right beside me encouraging me and sometimes carrying me in my weakness. Help me to trust that You have the best in mind for me. Amen.

FURTHER READING

2 Corinthians 10:3–6

Ephesians 6:10–19

Breaking Intimidation by John Bevere, Charisma House, 1995, 2006

Knowing God Intimately by Joyce Meyer, 2003, Time Warner Book Group, New York, NY.

CHAPTER FOURTEEN

NOW I SEE

I graduated from vision therapy in the early fall, so the eye exercises were no longer part of my daily life. I didn't miss them at all. It was a trying time, but I won that battle and was given an appointment card for six months down the road. I could focus perfectly, look at a computer without feeling nauseated, walk without bouncing off the walls, and close my eyes without feeling like I was on an angle. I could see better than when I started, both close up and from a distance. My brain was re-trained. I had completed something. The sense of accomplishment felt good and gave me the strength I'd need to complete the next phase of treatment.

At the end of vision therapy, I asked the doctor if I could try contact lenses again, and he gave me some to try. It turned out to be a very interesting experience. I put them in and went about my days as usual. I started having recurring pain that I hadn't had for quite some time. At this point in my process, I could tell when I was going to suffer the consequences of my actions. I knew something different was happening.

When I went for my appointment to see Joy, I lay down on the table, and she immediately asked me what I'd been doing. My cranial system had shut down; everything was tight and immovable. I told her that the only thing different was the contact lenses. Who knew that changing from glasses to contact lenses could do that to a person's head? We both learned something that day. I went home, and the contact lenses went into the garbage. I was back to wearing two pairs of glasses ... when I could find them.

It's fascinating how our brain works—what it will adapt to and what it won't. I've discovered, through trial and error, that my brain cannot handle the same stimulation as it did before it was traumatized. I don't really like loud and noisy places with lots of action or lights; I like quiet and low lights at night. It's funny that I can still handle loud music, though. It must be because that's my favourite.

Sometimes I feel overwhelmed, and that's okay; most times I can find a quiet place and just sit until that feeling goes away. The problem arises when I don't recognize what's going on, and I get angry before I can get away. It's not the same anger as when you're angry at someone. For example, someone might ask me a question, and I may not be able to answer if I'm overwhelmed, so I snap at them. Afterwards, I wonder why and feel bad. I've become somewhat of an expert at apologizing. I seem to get lots and lots of practice.

I continued in the "rest" season, becoming more accustomed to a less active lifestyle. I still had pain every day, but gradually it became less. I stopped taking pain medication regularly and chose to let my body tell me when to stop and rest. I was sleeping much better and had finally caught up from the sleep deprivation I'd experienced three years prior. My jaw continued to heal, even though some days it liked to make itself known above the other pain. For the most part, I could tolerate the aches and pain that were still my constant companions. I knew that if I was obedient and kept my physical activities to a bare minimum, I'd continue to heal. Joy was pleased with my progress. I started to enjoy the times when I could sit or recline and take my head off my shoulders, so-to-speak, because it didn't hurt at all. The more I rested, the less I felt pain.

Joy was finally able to do some major adjusting of my head bones, and the pain in my head and behind my eyes lessened considerably. I could also read for longer periods of time. I had a scheduled check-up with the eye specialist in the spring and was looking forward to seeing how I was doing. I told him my eyes ached a lot of the time, mostly because I'd developed a bad habit of looking under my distance glasses to read or see closer objects.

Eventually, I stopped wearing my glasses in the house altogether, because I could see well enough without them. I was straining my eyes and eye muscles by going from one extreme to another. I didn't like changing glasses all the time, and usually my reading glasses were nowhere to be found. I couldn't wear either pair around my neck because of the strain from the weight. I didn't have a solution to the problem, but my eye specialist did. Woo Hoo! He told me about a fairly new technology for making lenses that would give me a wider range of vision through multi-vision. He had two patients who had tried them; one adjusted with no problem, and one did not. Fifty-fifty odds ... I was in!

Two weeks later I picked up my new stylish glasses, and immediately I could see much clearer. I could read, and within a day I didn't have any eye strain or eye ache, and my eyes weren't as sensitive to the light. God is good! I had new vision, and I really could see the world differently. There aren't enough words to express how I felt now that I had some permanent glasses—another thing that had been completed.

VISION

Vision:

1. the ability to see: sight or eyesight;
2. something that you imagine: a picture that you see in your mind;
3. something that you see or dream especially as part of a religious or supernatural experience.

Most of us take for granted the ability to see. If we have sight, we use it and don't usually think too much about it. When my head was traumatized and my vision became skewed, I was confused and didn't know how to correctly process what I was seeing. There was nothing wrong with my eyes. My problem originated in my brain ... in my occipital lobe, to be precise. I was off-balance and had focusing and cognitive issues.

Isn't this what happens to all of us when we encounter trauma? It wounds us, and then we see the world through the skewed vision the trauma produces. Just as I retrained my brain through daily eye exercises, we can renew our minds so that we don't see everything through the hurt and wounds of trauma. God wants our vision to be aligned to His, to what He sees in us and what we see through Him. Before we can truly help others, we must see ourselves as God sees us. We can only do this by finding out who our Father God is; we are made in His image, and we resemble Him. After all, we are His children. Who we are is determined by what the Father shows us and what we believe about ourselves. Then we can reproduce what we believe to those in our world. The Bible says that without vision, people perish (Proverbs 29:18), and that's what God wants to give us—eyes to see the true vision of ourselves.

Within each of us is a destiny that God formed in us while we were in our mother's womb. Just because we have trauma doesn't mean His plan for us has changed. He knows the beginning from the end. He already knew what we were going to go through.

As we move through the process of becoming who we were made to be, we'll develop a clearer vision of what God has for us. That's what retraining our brain and renewing our mind is all about—it enables us to know more of who we really are. With God's perspective and His vision, we'll start to see the good in people, and that each one is a diamond waiting to sparkle and shine. We can ask for God's perspective, and then it's our responsibility to believe.

Often we need healing of a trauma and its effects before we can believe. That's okay—Jesus is in the business of healing. Once we believe, we can see where we're going, even if some of the steps aren't quite visible yet and we can't see all the way to the end. God asks the same question several times in the Bible: What do you see? Our vision is limited to what's right in front of us, but God sees beyond all we can ever imagine and think. Maybe it's time to ask Him to show you what He sees, and then step into a lifetime of adventure and wonder where the dreams He has placed in you come alive. Remember, nothing is impossible when you're connected to God.

GOING DEEPER

REFLECTION

1. Where is your vision skewed in how you see yourself and situations?

2. Where might you have a wound because of trauma?

3. God wants to heal our wounds from traumatic experiences. Ask Him to come into that wound and heal it.

4. Ask God to show you how He sees you.

DECREE

Don't let your hearts be troubled. Trust in God, and trust also in me. (John 14:1) "For I know the plans I have for you," says the LORD. "They are plans for good and not for disaster, to give you a future and a hope." (Jeremiah 29:11) But you are the ones chosen by God, chosen for the high calling of priestly work, chosen to be a holy people, God's instruments to do his work and speak out for him, to tell others of the night-and-day difference he made for you—from nothing to something, from rejected to accepted. (1 Peter 2:9–10, MSG).

PRAYER

Father, help me to see what You see. I want to have Your vision so I can live the full, abundant life Jesus died to give me. I need a change of perspective of myself and others. I know that hurting people hurt others, and I don't want to hurt those I love anymore. Give me new vision for a new season in my life. Breathe on me, Holy Spirit, and awaken my spiritual vision so I can see the illuminated path before me. I don't want to settle for less than what You have designed me to be in this life. I want to walk in the future and hope You have for me. In Jesus' precious name. Amen.

FURTHER READING

Mark 8:22–25

Jeremiah 1:11–12

Extraordinary by John Bevere, 2009, published by Waterbrook Press, Colorado Springs, Colorado

CHAPTER FIFTEEN

BRAIN TALK

With my vision cleared, I began to focus on my shoulders. They were still tense, so I used a portable machine designed to send electrical pulses to specific areas (TENS) for pain. Because I had another appointment with Joy coming up, I kept doing what I knew to do and waited to see what she would tell me. At my appointment, I asked her if my shoulders would ever get better. Every time I held my arms in the air for more than a few minutes, my shoulders began to feel over-extended and would begin aching. It wasn't getting any better with time. She explained that my muscles had been released enough that they could relax, but my brain was so used to my shoulders being tense, it had forgotten how to make those muscles relax. That was fascinating to me. How could my brain forget something that had come so naturally all my life? This was wonderful news, because it meant something could be done about it. I was going to tell my brain to relax my shoulder muscles until it learned to do it naturally on its own.

I went home with the good news. I didn't have a plan yet, but I knew one would come. I met with Pastor C. the next day and told her what I had learned; she immediately helped me with a strategy for success. I put sticky notes up in strategic places, and when I saw them, I made my shoulders relax. More self-discipline was needed for me to move forward. I seemed to constantly be pulling my shoulders down. I couldn't remember to relax unless I saw the notes, because my brain had forgotten and couldn't remind me. I woke up a couple of weeks later and realized that my shoulders were tense. I'd scrunched up my muscles while I was sleeping. I forced those babies down and sat there for five minutes, not moving. They were going to get this whether they wanted to or not! I worked every day at pushing them down and retraining my brain so that eventually they could relax on their own.

My shoulders started getting better—not perfect, but they didn't ache all the time and there was definitely less tension. I was learning to relax. Now that my shoulders were being re-programmed, I had more pain-free times during the day and, although my physical activity didn't change much, I felt a lot better. Usually I could control my shoulders and get them to relax, but there were times when they hurt a lot. Even though I wanted to know why this was happening, I left it alone for the moment and enjoyed the times my body didn't scream in pain.

Feeling better came with the guilt that I should be doing more. Where was that sense of accomplishment I desired to feel at the end of the day? I didn't let myself go into a state of discouragement, but kept pushing forward; however, that feeling of not getting anything done grew. It progressed to the point where I was so focused on getting things done, I wasn't getting anything done at all. I seemed to be going from one thing to another, not finishing what I started. When I'd go back to what I didn't get done, I'd feel guilty and worthless.

The cycle continued for a couple of weeks until I went to see Joy for my scheduled appointment. When she checked my body before starting, she announced that I had turned a corner.

I received this good news ecstatically. We talked about endorphins and cortisol while she did the stretching and moving of the bones in my head, and I told her about the bouts of pain from my shoulder muscles. She mentioned that when I was excited and happy, I'd put my whole body into expressing those emotions. As a result, my muscles would tense, I'd talk faster, and my arms would be very involved in my explanations. My muscles would involuntarily tense up, and my body would release cortisol to counteract the stress this placed on my body. I probably had done this all my life, but now that my muscles were compromised and needed to relax to heal, it affected me adversely. Bottom line: My happy emotions were hurting me. It was disappointing and fascinating all at the same time. She told me to get a natural stress relief spray that's been around for years to help calm me when I got over-excited. She also gave me "becalm" balls to lie my head on every day for about ten minutes to help keep my body in a relaxed state. I now had some tools to use and felt like she enabled me to move forward.

At my appointment with Pastor C., we talked about the revelation I had received from Joy. She assured me it was not normal for our happy emotions to harm us, and also that there was a solution to this issue. Just as I had received strategy for healing in other areas, God was faithful and I would get an answer this time as well. She mentioned meditation. This had been mentioned to me before, but I couldn't relax enough to do it. Imagine that! Now I was determined to do it, because I could see how it would benefit me and help me to further relax.

A group of us were getting prepared to go on a mission trip to Honduras during this time. I was having difficulty accepting the fact that I was to go, but I continued to prepare and didn't think about it too much. As the trip got closer and more details came out, I realized there would be little sleep during the first three days of the journey. There would be many bus rides on bumpy roads, and it would be hot and humid because it was their rainy season. This made it a little harder not to think about the trip, but I used the spray, laid on the becalm balls, and meditated.

About fifty of us—all Canadians—left that summer with about 1,450 other missionaries from the United States to invade Honduras with the love of God. It was a trip of a lifetime. Yes, there was minimal sleep the first three days. Yes, there were bumpy bus rides for three to four hours each way every day. Yes, it was hot and humid, but there was a heat wave at home and it was hotter there than in Honduras. It hardly rained and, most importantly, I survived and actually enjoyed myself. God's amazing grace covered me, and He proved to me yet again that He's right there beside me. While I was there, I had many opportunities to practice relaxing!

When I got home I had another appointment with Joy. We talked more about my body releasing cortisol. I was intrigued and wanted to know the effects of this chemical. It's known as the "fight or flight" chemical, so if you're in danger, it releases into your system so you have the energy needed to run away from that danger. It's also released when your physical body is under stress and you don't know how to relieve that stress. When there's no actual threat, it can manifest as a hunger for food. This piece of information made me sit up and take notice. This was happening to me. I'd feel hungry at times right after I ate if my body was under physical stress, but of course I didn't know that was the reason. This was more incentive to get my body trained to relax.

I met again with Pastor C. and uncovered that my body was unwilling to co-operate with my will. If I wanted to experience success in the area of emotional control, I was going to have to speak to my body and tell it to line up with the way God made it to function. This may sound odd to you, but people talk to plants all the time and tell them to grow. Why not tell your body to do what it was made to do? I believe that something happens when you release words into the atmosphere, and when you hear them you must react. It reminds me of the old saying: "Sticks and stones may break my bones but words can never hurt me." Lie, lie, lie! Words linger far longer than we realize. I decided I could use words in a positive way to get my emotions to line up. I also started talking to my muscles and told them to line up too. I added my nerves, tendons, ligaments, bones, brain, and my mind. I decreed a full body alignment. It seemed to work, so I kept doing it.

MIND/BRAIN CONNECTION

Spirit: The force within a person that is believed to give the body life, energy, and power.

Soul:
1. the spiritual part of a person that is believed to give life to the body and, in many religions, is believed to live forever;
2. a person's deeply felt moral and emotional nature.

Body: person's or animal's whole physical self.

We are all created with a spirit, soul, and body. This is what differentiates us from animals, and this is why we haven't evolved. It's what makes us human and connects us all. We are born separated from the God, who created us through the avenue of our parents, so our spirits are dead to God. When we ask Jesus into our heart, our spirit becomes alive to God and we enter the family of God; we become sons and daughters, and we have a Father. We were designed to operate in God's order of spirit, soul, and body. Our spirit is perfect, because it is the Spirit of Jesus, the mind of Christ. Unfortunately, our souls are used to ruling our lives.

Our soul consists of our mind, will, and emotions. They don't change when we give our lives to Jesus. Actually, our souls are at enmity with God, and the battle begins to bring our souls in line with what the Spirit of God says about us. We spend our whole lives aligning our soul with the mind of Christ in us. This is done by renewing our mind, so it lines up with what God says about us. Our body is last in line, and it was created to follow along behind our soul and do what it's told. When we get it in the wrong order, we don't experience growth, but instead we become discouraged and angry. We were created for our spirit to lead, our soul to line up with our spirit, and our body to follow along. Because God made our body as His temple, you can be assured He wants us to take care of it too.

When I first discovered I had a spirit that needed to be taken care of, I plunged into deep waters. I began to study about the things of the spirit, learning about good and bad angels, spirits in me trying to rule me, and principalities and authorities in high places. This fascinated me. I spent a lot of time learning about this aspect of a world I knew nothing about when I came into the Kingdom of God. I also discovered I had a soul that was at odds with God. It wanted to have its own way all the time. When I decided to follow God, I was at constant war with my soul and the teachings in the Bible, because my soul was connected to the things of this world. I always said the world had left me lame and had nothing I wanted anymore, but sometimes my actions proved otherwise. Wanting to change was a far cry far from making it happen, and in order to get the results that would bring me peace, I had to make some changes. I had to activate my will and go into battle with my soul, one day at a time.

I had this wrong mindset that God wasn't really interested in my physical body, even though I am a three-part being: spirit, soul, and body. I left the body part out, and although it looked like I took care of myself, I was struggling on the inside. After my car accident, something deep inside of me took control, and I pushed to get better. When I didn't get the result I was looking for, I pushed and strived more instead of stopping and asking for help. God was letting me come to the end of myself. I was caught in a cycle of wrong thinking: *I can make myself better. I can do this.* This was all happening while I was in training as a disciple and when I was trying to be open and share what I was going through—as much as I was able to understand about myself at that time. I was covered with a veil of deception, which produced denial that there was anything wrong with my physical body. That denial caused me to continue to push myself to my limit every day, when what my body really needed was an abundance of rest.

I can save you a lot of grief and pain if you'll receive and believe that we are created as a three-part being, and that God is concerned about every part of us. He wants us to walk in freedom as a whole body so that we can have peace and joy while we're on earth. Life is a gift. I am learning every day how precious, unique, and absolutely perfect God has made me. Trauma of all types veiled the true, beautiful me, but when Jesus removed the veil, I only needed to believe and receive. The darkness of this wrong mindset has been revealed, and I refuse to fight the battle of the restoration of my physical body alone. Since my spirit has been awakened to God, and the veil of this deception has been removed, I'm free to treat my body as a living temple. The pride that stopped me from humbling myself under the hand of God has been found out and bound. I will not serve my body; my body will serve me.

Are you caught in the trap of not taking care of your body? Have you compromised your spiritual well-being by focusing too much on your physical body? Is your soul leading you down paths you don't really want to go, but you don't know how to stop? If you want to make some changes, be honest with yourself and allow God to reveal why you do what you do. Then you can make changes by activating your will and asking God to help you. Spend some time sitting quietly and listening to your thoughts, writing what you are thinking, and then replacing the negative thoughts with the positive thoughts found in the Word of God.

It's so simple, it seems difficult. When we acknowledge God's order for our whole being, we will understand that the Spirit in us is perfect. Because of this, we want to line our soul up with our spirit and tell our body how to behave. Our brain is like a computer, and we can tell it what to do. We can retrain it by telling it that it doesn't like those things that hurt us. We can create good habits by using our wills and speaking to our mind, which is now lining up with the mind of Christ. Acting out of that new mind (our new nature), instead of our emotions, we can do anything with God.

GOING DEEPER

REFLECTION

1. How well do you take care of your body? Are there areas that you need to reconsider?

2. It's important to take care of all the parts of your being—spirit, soul, and body. Have you been neglecting any of these areas? If so, which ones?

3. Are there certain behaviours you aren't able to stop doing? How can choosing to take care of your spirit, soul, or body help this? What steps can you take?

DECREE

Let the words of my mouth and the meditation of my heart be acceptable in your sight, O LORD, my rock and my redeemer. (Psalm 19:14, ESV) I will study your commandments and reflect on your ways. (Psalm 119:15) My child, pay attention to what I say. Listen carefully to my words. Don't lose sight of them. Let them penetrate deep into your heart, for they bring life to those who find them, and healing to their whole body. (Proverbs 4:20–22) You will keep in perfect peace all who trust in you, all whose thoughts are fixed on you! (Isaiah 26:3)

PRAYER

Father, I come to You broken, but I will be unashamed as I ask for Your help. Pride has kept me from asking for help which You freely give, and I repent of pride. I want to be whole—spirit, soul, and body—so I can have the peace and joy that Jesus died to give me. Reveal any hurts and wounds that keep me in this cycle of abuse and which ultimately affect others. I am tired and weak, and my heart's desire is to be strong and awake. Nothing is impossible for You, God. I receive and believe all You have for me. In Jesus' name I pray. Amen.

FURTHER READING

Philippians 4:4–9

Psalm 1

Switch on Your Brain by Dr. Caroline Leaf, Baker, 2013

The Forgotten Way Meditations by Ted Dekker, Ted Dekker Copyright, 2015

Victorious Emotions by Wendy Backlund, Igniting Hope Ministries, 2017

CHAPTER SIXTEEN

LOOSEN UP AND STRETCH OUT

I continued telling my body to align. I was meditating, lying on balls that calmed me, and stretching and relaxing during this time. I had a much busier life taking care of myself than I could ever have imagined. While doing all this, I ended up at a plateau again. Everything seemed to be staying the same—not at a bad spot, but not moving forward to the wholeness I desired. My next appointment with Joy revealed more strategy for me if I chose to use it. Being the overachiever that I am, and because I so desperately wanted to be whole, I took the strategy and pushed forward.

I had no idea an ordinary tennis ball could cause so much pain. I was to put the tennis ball against a wall and line it up about an inch from my spine. Slowly, ever so slowly, I was to let it run up and down my spine on both sides while leaning against it. OUCH, OUCH, OUCH! The first day I was in tears and had nausea so bad I had to sit down after completing the exercise. The muscles along my spine were so tight, even the slightest pressure on them hurt like crazy. I finished one side of my spine, and then realized I had to do the other one too. It was very painful. I didn't like it at all, but I could tell it was exactly what was needed if I wanted more healing.

After the first two days, I hardly noticed my back, because my legs hurt so much from all the squatting I was doing. I liked this part, because I always wanted to get my legs back into some sort of shape besides lumpy, but even that hurt. No pain, no gain. I was now up to a forty-five-minute workout every morning before I did anything else for the day.

LOOSENING AND STRETCHING

Loosen: to release from restraint.

Stretch: to become extended without breaking.

God is always moving forward, and He wants us to move with Him at the pace He sets for our lives, but it is our choice to make. It may seem like we're not moving at all sometimes, but that's a lie the enemy wants us to believe. God is faithful to show signs of movement for those with eyes to see. He is constantly moving us so that those things that hold us back will loosen. When He has given us a little shaking, we'll be more flexible and able to move with Him.

When we first start that loosening process it's usually painful. Loosening my spine muscles hurt a lot at the beginning, but now (as long as I'm consistent) it feels good to run that ball up and down my back. It keeps me flexible and allows all the fluid that runs through my spine to have room to ebb and flow. Loosening is just another word for freedom. When you taste the benefits of freedom, you to want more.

Long before I started loosening with the tennis ball, I stretched. It got to the point where I plateaued, because stretching didn't benefit me anymore without first loosening the muscles. God wants to stretch us all. He likes to see us move into what He has for us. He wants to see us step into our destiny, to move us out of our comfort zone into the adventure zone with Him. That can only go so far before we need to allow Him to loosen and shake some things off us so we can know more of who He is and who we are. Sometimes we move ahead and want to discover who we are without involving Him, but that doesn't release us into the best He has for us. We end up settling for a form of godliness without the power (2 Timothy 3:5) because we refuse to let Him loosen our hurts and wounds. Once we allow Him access, He will stretch us further by sending us out into our world equipped to advance His Kingdom.

It's a beautiful thing to see someone walking the path God has made for them and growing into who God has made them to be. When you feel like you're stuck, allow God to shake things up and loosen a bit of that extra baggage you may be carrying around on your back. It's an adventurous life discovering who you really are. He wants to make us strong, and strength isn't determined by how much we carry with us through life by worrying and fretting, but by the joy we have in our life.

Ask God to loosen and shake you, and then stretch you into who you were made to be. Cast your cares on Jesus; His yoke is easy, and His burden is light (1 Peter 5:11; Matthew 11:30). You will be filled with joy, and you'll be a much stronger person than you ever thought possible.

GOING DEEPER

REFLECTION

1. Are you carrying burdens you need to release and let go of in order to grow? Make a list.

2. Do you feel tired and weak? Can you identify where you feel that way?

3. Are there areas where you know you are being stretched? Ask Holy Spirit to show you your part in the process.

DECREE

Are you tired? Worn out? Burned out on religion? Come to me. Get away with me and you'll recover your life. I'll show you how to take a real rest. Walk with me and work with me—watch how I do it. Learn the unforced rhythms of grace. I won't lay anything heavy or ill-fitting on you. Keep company with me and you'll learn to live freely and lightly. (Matthew 11:28–30, MSG) Each time he said, "My grace is all you need. My power works best in weakness." So now I am glad to boast about my weaknesses, so that the power of Christ can work through me. That's why I take pleasure in my weaknesses, and in the insults, hardships, persecutions, and troubles that I suffer for Christ. For when I am weak, then I am strong.

(2 Corinthians 12:9-10) Don't be dejected and sad, for the joy of the LORD is your strength! (Nehemiah 8:10b) Enlarge your house. You are going to need a bigger place; don't underestimate the amount of room that you'll need. So build, build, build. (Isaiah 54:2, VOICE)

PRAYER

Dear Father, I feel like I'm stuck and I can't see any movement towards the freedom the Bible promises for me. Show me how to be free. Show me how to release my cares to You and receive the joy You have for me! Shake off the burdens of my life that I am carrying. Loosen the garments I have placed on myself that are not from You. I want to be strong in You. In Jesus' name. Amen.

FURTHER READING

Psalm 27:5–7

Hebrews 3, 4, 12

Set Yourself Free, Expanded Edition by Robert Heidler, Glory of Zion International Ministries, 2010

CHAPTER SEVENTEEN

PAIN

My life at this point was not one of ease. Most mornings I awoke to discouragement knocking on my door. Time well spent with Jesus every morning allowed me to push discouragement out, and when I chose to stay connected with my Lord, I had a day of peace and contentment, regardless of the pain. I've had several inner conversations with God about pain, and although I still must deal with it, I push forward with the knowledge that God always offers relief while I'm waiting for deliverance.

I've come to the conclusion that there are two basic types of pain. There is the pain of trauma and the pain of recovery. Although pain takes many different forms, the root cause can be summed up as one of these two. The pain of trauma includes all the physical and emotional hurts and wounds of the past that left a mark on us and changed us. We never remain the same after a trauma, whether small or large; we are forever marked by that moment in time. What we do with those wounds determines if we remain in the pain of the trauma or move on to the pain of recovery. When I moved to the recovery pain, I didn't realize it was recovery pain because my brain still acknowledged the pain the same way. I had issues!

When you decide to co-operate with God and yield to His way of doing things, you enter into recovery pain. You must abandon what you've been doing that isn't working, because it keeps you in a cycle of trauma pain. This made me fearful, because I was familiar with the pain of the trauma. This recovery pain was new territory, and I didn't know how to respond. I didn't realize that as I moved forward, regardless of fear, I moved into a new level of maturity in my walk with God. As I stepped into the pain of recovery, I stepped out in faith. My boundaries seemed very small, and physically they were. I felt very restricted, and the road seemed very narrow.

The recovery path from trauma is a lonely path when you take the first step. No one but God knows how you feel. I couldn't put into words the emotional and physical hurt I was feeling, but I knew that I didn't want to go back and I couldn't stay where I was, because it hurt too much. I was in a position to make the right choice. You must take the time alone with God and examine yourself when you get to that crossroad. Take a good look at your situation in a real way, not the way you pretend it to be. No cover-ups. Ask God for the courage to remove the blanket.

I believe we go into recovery pain every time we examine ourselves, choose to face reality, and deal with the trauma in our life. It feels like recovery pain after surgery. When you wake up it hurts a lot. Then you go home and rest, and every day you do a little more and feel a little better. Before you know it, you're feeling better than you did before the surgery. Even though you may need to adjust, if you change the way you do things, you continue to feel well. The key is change. If you're not willing to change the way you do things when you enter into recovery, you'll go back to the familiar pain of the trauma. Changing our attitude and our way of doing things at God's direction is the way to move from recovery into the wholeness we all desire.

CHOOSE TO CHANGE

> Change: to undergo transformation, transition, or substitution.

I chose to change. I chose to face the pain of trauma from past hurts and wounds in my life and allow God in, so that pain could serve me. I chose not to serve the pain.

My pain wasn't just from the car accident. When I chose to let God in, He wanted to heal all the hurts and wounds I'd held onto in my soul. That pain from trauma had built up over the years, and now because of the car accident, I was placed in a position to choose to move from the pain of trauma to the pain of recovery. They both hurt, and at first I didn't have the discernment to know I'd actually shifted from one to the other. With lots of help from my mentor, I made this shift when I said yes to God. It still hurt, but as I moved forward with God, the pain was of a different nature. I worked with Holy Spirit to loosen and release those wounds that had festered, infecting me and others throughout my life.

God will often bring us to crossroads in our lives. There's no escaping it, but because He loves us, He encourages us to make our own decision as to what road we will take. He never said there wouldn't be pain and suffering in this life. We live in a fallen world, and satan comes to kill, steal, and destroy. When we choose a path not formed by the Lord, we allow satan access to our souls. All may seem well for a while, but satan hates us and wants us to suffer trauma pain for all eternity. Jesus, on the other hand, came to set the captives free. When we follow Him, we enter into recovery pain, because He turns everything around for our best. Knowing we're in recovery pain helps us break through into victory, conquering satan and his plans for us.

We cannot change ourselves. Sometimes we think behaviour modification creates lasting change, but when situations start stacking on top of each other and we have used self-will, we'll eventually fold. Effectual change for our benefit can only be created by God when we co-operate with Holy Spirit through obedience and spending time in His presence. For years I thought I could change myself by trying harder. It appeared to work ... until I had a car accident and couldn't "fix" what was wrong with me by "doing." It was so much work!

God has made it so simple for us. When you come to a crossroad, examine where you are and face the reality of your situation. Take an honest look at yourself and then choose to move forward with God. Obey Holy Spirit, spend time in the presence of God, and watch Him change you into who you were meant to be—the real you who will live with Jesus in Heaven for all eternity.

GOING DEEPER

REFLECTION

1. Are you at a crossroad right now?

2. What are the realities of your situation? Write them down.

3. Pain can be emotional, physical, or both. What pain are you experiencing?

DECREE

And so, dear brothers and sisters, I plead with you to give your bodies to God because of all he has done for you. Let them be a living and holy sacrifice—the kind he will find acceptable. This is truly the way to worship him. Don't copy the behavior and customs of this world, but let God transform you into a new person by changing the way you think. Then you will learn to know God's will for you, which is good and pleasing and perfect. (Romans 12:1–2) For God has not given us a spirit of fear and timidity, but of power, love, and self-discipline (2 Timothy 1:7) But for you who fear my name, the Sun of Righteousness will rise with healing in his wings. And you will go free, leaping with joy like calves let out to pasture (Malachi 4:2) And I am certain that God, who began the good work within you, will continue his work until it is finally finished on the day when Christ Jesus returns (Philippians 1:6)

PRAYER

Father, I thank You for making me who I am. I want to move out of any destructive cycle where I am stuck in trauma pain. I want to move forward into recovery pain so I can receive all You have for me. Holy Spirit, please give me courage to take a step of faith towards You and what You have for me. I choose to change. I choose to allow You into my heart to heal the hurts that sit there in darkness. I ask for the glory light of Jesus to come heal my heart. Show me Your ways, Jesus. Amen.

FURTHER READING

2 Corinthians 3:7–18

1 John 3:1–3

Psalm 139

2 Timothy 1:7–10

The Rewards of Simplicity by Pam and Chuck D. Pierce, Chosen Books, 2010

CHAPTER EIGHTEEN

FAITH TO BELIEVE

Adjustment, change, and trials weren't just in my body—they seemed to be in every area of my life. The company we'd started wasn't getting work. We received the bad news from our customers that we wouldn't be getting any orders in the foreseeable future. We were caught in the slump of the manufacturing industry, and business came to an abrupt halt. This was not what we'd expected, and because we were a new business, we weren't prepared to carry on through to the spring. When we didn't have work, we didn't get paid, and it was the Christmas season. It could have been a very dismal time for us, but we chose to keep moving forward, buckle down, and spend as little as possible so we could survive until the spring. I had the opportunity to use all the skills I'd learned up to this point: relaxing, trusting, and relaxing some more. I did a lot of deep breathing during that time. I wouldn't let all those negative thoughts invade my mind. As soon as they entered, I told them to move on out, and I focused my energy on the Spirit of Christmas—Jesus. I would not let the enemy ruin my Christmas.

I was born a warrior, but I'm not perfect. Sometimes I rely on my own, man-made armour. Sometimes I can be a princess, because that's part of who I am, but I am a princess warrior bride, and usually I have my pretty white bridal dress tucked safely under my armour. The armour of God covers me (Ephesians 6:11).

At times I've denied the warrior in me, thinking I'm too abrupt, but I realize that this is who God made me to be. I was born for such a time as this. I really like action movies, especially where good beats the living daylights out of evil. The reason I've shoved my warrior down a bit is because I know that some of the ways I fight are not God's way... they're my way.

God has been teaching me my princess side by showing me who I am in Christ. He didn't need to let me know I was a warrior—I'd been fighting my whole life for my rights and my way, but He brought to life my feminine side. After all, I am a girl, and I like girly things too. I definitely needed to learn that it's okay to have emotions and show them. We all have them, and they are from God. I'm still learning and will continue to learn throughout my life about myself and who I am. That being said, I cannot be little Miss Muffet who sat on her tuffet eating her curds and whey, because along came that spider that sat down beside her and frightened Miss Muffet away. I like food, and no spider is going to get my food. I will not be frightened away by fear.

I must learn how to use the weapons God has given me. I like to imagine what they look like. Mine are big and sharp and pointy. I believe the weapons God wants me to unwrap further are faith, hope, and love. Unusual weapons in this world, but not unusual where I come from ... my homeland. These are the weapons of Heaven.

I remember struggling through some issues, and all I kept hearing was the word "delay." I entrusted a few people with this word, and continued to push through, believing that God would reveal something to someone. He did, and I learned I had fear, mistrust, and unbelief all working together. A three-cord strand is hard to break (Ecclesiastes 4:12). The Lord said this was the delay, and that faith, hope, and love would break that strand. The greatest of these is love.

When we struggled to believe that God had a good plan for our business, I prayed in desperation, because we didn't know what to do or which way to go. We were at a crossroad. I wrote out one of my prayers: "Faith to believe for the miracle we need is harder today. The air feels thick with unbelief, and pulling on the faith in Heaven and dragging it down to earth to mix with my faith seems like an impossible feat. Since God works with our faith, not our need, I must retain and stir up my faith, although it does seem like that small mustard seed today. But stirred up it joins with the faith in Heaven, because it's all faith up there. That extra faith I need down here is up there. In Heaven, nothing is impossible. Doors are opened, and we just walk through. In Heaven, there is peace amidst the waves of the storm that seem never ending. Oh God of the universe, help me to believe that You know what is best and that You bring every good and perfect gift to me to the glory of Your name!

"Help me be strong in faith to believe that a miracle, no matter what it looks like, is coming into the mess that is my life at this moment. God, I look to You. I won't be overwhelmed. Give me Your vision to see things like You do. God, I look to You give me wisdom. You know what we should do. Release the wisdom and revelation, Lord, so we know what to do. Please lay the path straight, and clear the obstacles that are blocking the way. Release the angels we need to push us through this tight spot into the wide-open green pasture You have for us. Stir our faith to believe that You are the miracle-maker. One word from Your mouth changes everything. We have placed our Isaac on the altar, and we have that knife raised up to sacrifice. Will you provide the sacrifice and save this business?"

God answered by writing back to me (even though I wrote it). The answer He gave me is written under "Faith, Hope, and Love" in the next section. He released faith so we could believe He had a good plan for our business. After that day, I realized that even if the business shut its doors, we'd be just fine. We waited and listened, and when Holy Spirit told us specific strategies to move forward, we did what He said and felt peace beyond our own understanding.

FAITH, HOPE, AND LOVE

Faith:
1. strong belief or trust in someone or something;
2. belief in the existence of God: strong religious feelings or beliefs.

Hope: to expect with confidence.

Love: unselfish, loyal, and benevolent concern for the good of another as: (1) the fatherly concern of God for humankind; (2) brotherly concern for others.

The battle belongs to the Lord, and He is the One who brings us the victory when we follow His instructions. He continues to teach me that I have already won the battle. I don't need to fight without His help. We don't fight against flesh and blood, but against powers and principalities and every high thing that sets itself up against God (Ephesians 6:12). We fight from a place of victory by using His weapons that allow Him to be made known to the world. His weapons are faith, hope, and love.

How can I possibly love without the hope of receiving the love I must give? How can I hope to know the lover of my soul without the faith to believe? My love at most will be an extension of what I think it should be if I don't first receive the love of the Father into my heart. Without having the hope of things to come—the hope of Heaven and miracles—I will not pursue the love of the Father. The hope I have will turn into hopelessness if I don't activate the faith I've been given. My faith grows as I believe, move into the hope of Christ, and receive the love of the Father. Receiving that love creates an atmosphere for miracles. I only need the faith of that tiny mustard seed. That faith will cause me to believe for the miracle I need. In faith—real faith—I will obey God, because I believe what He says, and when I obey, I activate my faith.

Once my faith is activated, I can hope for the impossible, because my faith now has action. At this stage, we must continue to believe and obey in faith, because faith without works is dead. As we continue to believe and obey, our faith continues to grow, and our hope stays right where it needs to be, knowing we are doing our part to keep hope alive by believing and obeying. This activates our faith and keeps us moving forward to the next step in God's order— love.

Before we can truly love others the way Jesus did, we must receive the love of the Father. In faith, we hope for those things not seen in the natural. We pray for answers to situations and seek wisdom and vision. They are all attained by spending quality time in the presence of God, so He can change our hearts to line up with His. Then He can pour His love into us, and we can pour out His love to others. This is a wonderful God-cycle for miracles.

When we lack faith, we don't obey God, and then it's impossible to please Him! This is where we start striving. We want to please God, but we want to do it our way ... take a shortcut around the mountain when God wants us to go over it. Sometimes we feel so far from what God wants, we try almost anything to get "back in the good books" with Him. We must go back to the place where we disconnected and then repent and change from our ways to His way and start from there.

Once we get back on His righteous path, we have the faith to believe and our hope is truly activated, resulting in hope for a better future. Hope is needed for something not yet seen, for something better in the future. Activated faith produces hope that is backed by the Word of God. When we obey what God has told us and begin to hope, we can speak into our atmosphere the things we hope for. Whether we see it or not, something changes. Something miraculous happens, and that's when our miracle begins.

According to God's Word, the love aspect of this cycle is the greatest (1 Corinthians 13:13). Without the love of God, we are human beings just like every other human being. We are limited to loving conditionally. We cannot love the unlovable without God's love poured into us. We must make room for this love, as we cannot comprehend it with our natural minds. I need faith to believe and obey, to activate hope for things unseen. With that hope, I put myself in a position to receive the love of the Father that I need for each situation. The only way I can feel peace and be able to say I am counting all my trials as joy is by stepping into the love of the Father. It's the presence of God that pushes me through that tight place to the greener pastures. It's a calm assurance of knowing that God is in control and that He has a plan. All mistrust, fear, and unbelief are gone, because my Daddy has me covered. I sit under the shadow of His wings, where He fills me up with His love.

The Bible says:

> *If I speak God's Word with power, revealing all His mysteries and making everything plain as day, and if I have faith that says to a mountain, "Jump," and it jumps, but I don't love, I'm nothing. If I give everything I own to the poor, and even go to the stake to be burned as a martyr, but I don't love, I've gotten nowhere. So, no matter what I say, what I believe, and what I do, I'm bankrupt without love. Love never gives up. Love cares more for others than for self. Love doesn't want what it doesn't have. Love doesn't strut, doesn't have a swelled head, doesn't force itself on others, isn't always "me first," doesn't fly off the handle, doesn't keep score of the sins of others, doesn't revel when others grovel, takes pleasure in the flowering of truth, puts up with anything, trusts God always, always looks for the best, never looks back, but keeps going to the end.*
>
> —1 Corinthians 13:2–7, MSG

I cannot be any of those things without the love of the Father and without His presence. I have tried, strived, pushed, intimidated, and yelled what I thought was God's love, and it doesn't work. It's not His love; it's my conditional love, used to make me feel better. What does work is getting to that resting place, that secret place, and setting up camp there for as long as it takes, just soaking in His presence. Is it easy? Not for me. It takes practice. It takes turning the phone off. It takes locking the door. It takes saying "no" and spending the time needed. Satan doesn't want us to go there, so of course it's not easy. From this place of love, miracles happen, because the presence of God is with me and evident in me. Where I walk, atmospheres are changed. People change, and lives are brought into the Kingdom of God. Who wouldn't want to be in a kingdom where true love lives, rules, and reigns?

GOING DEEPER

REFLECTION

1. What are you hoping for?

2. What do you need to put into action to activate your faith? What steps do you need to take?

3. Share with someone you trust what you are hoping for. Pray together. Where there are two or more gathered in His name, He is there!

DECREE

So God's rest is there for people to enter, but those who first heard this good news failed to enter because they disobeyed God. So God set another time for entering his rest, and that time is today. God announced this through David much later in the words already quoted: "Today when you hear his voice, don't harden your hearts." (Hebrews 4:6–7) God is strong, and he wants you strong. So take everything the Master has set out for you, well-made weapons of the best materials. And put them to use so you will be able to stand up to everything the Devil throws your way. This is no afternoon athletic contest that we'll walk away from and forget about in a couple of hours. This is for keeps, a life-or-death fight to the finish against the Devil and all his angels. Be prepared. You're up against far more than you can handle on your own. Take all the help you can get, every weapon God has issued, so that when it's all over but the shouting you'll still be on your feet. Truth, righteousness, peace, faith, and salvation are more than words. Learn how to apply them. You'll need them throughout your life. God's Word is an indispensable weapon. In the same way, prayer is essential in this ongoing warfare. Pray hard and long. Pray for your brothers and sisters. Keep your eyes open. Keep each other's spirits up so that no one falls behind or drops out. (Ephesians 6:10–18, MSG) I tell you the truth, if you had faith even as small as a mustard seed, you could say to this mountain, "Move from here to there," and it would move. Nothing would be impossible. (Matthew 17:20)

PRAYER

I need to love like You love, Jesus. I know we've all been given a measure of faith, and I want to use my mustard seed size of faith to believe what You say is truth. I repent of unbelief, mistrust, and fear. Help me to believe. Help me to trust You. Give me the courage to step out in faith, to take a risk. Holy Spirit, come and fill me with Your presence so I may enter that place of rest that Jesus made available to me by going to the cross. Amen.

FURTHER READING

Hebrews 3 and 4

Mark 9:14–24

Matthew 7:7–9

James 1 (MSG)

Hosting His Presence by Bill Johnson, Destiny Image Publishers Inc., 2013

CHAPTER NINETEEN

WALK THE TALK

We made it through Christmas that year. Everyone enjoyed themselves, we ate too much, and we all had some gifts to open. My regular routine seemed to be thrown out the door and buried in the snow, so when the new year arrived, I started having frequent morning headaches and my jaw was tight and sore. My body needed the routine of exercise, stretching, and rest that it wasn't getting. This was when I realized that exercise was something I'd be doing the rest of my life.

When normality returned, I went to see Joy. My head was a mess. She adjusted me and said everything in my head went back to where it was supposed to be, but I needed to continue with my routine. We had created those new pathways, and in order for them to stay, I had to do my part to keep myself in the proper position. Watch out for the little foxes that spoil the vine (Song of Songs 2:15)! Failing to do those exercises and stretches added up, and I realized that I'd have to stick to these routines if I wanted to continue moving from recovery to wholeness. Not that I minded doing them, but some days I just didn't feel like it. This was the continuing separation of my emotions from my will. I decided I would do them regularly and

I would enjoy doing them, because doing those small things made a big difference in the whole picture of my life.

Joy mentioned adding another ball exercise to my daily routine that I'd been putting off because I was feeling pretty good and didn't want to start something new and have more pain. I was well versed in the effects of adding new exercises. My body was so sensitive, introducing anything new greatly affected how I functioned. In other words, I would experience pain. I wasn't excited to hear that I should start with my feet and that they would be "tender" for about a month. But I ordered the kit and determined to do these new exercises.

REVELATION AND RESPONSIBILITY

Revelation:

1. something that is revealed by God to humans;
2. an act of revealing or communicating divine truth.

Responsibility: something that you should do because it is morally right; legally required.

We must weigh the cost of moving forward from here, because once we move on, there will be no way to get back to this spot. Once I go through that door from here to there, it's going to shut behind me. Once I know something, I become responsible for doing something with it. It's an individual decision, because the fiery trials are unique to us. You don't know what I go through, and I can't possibly know all of what you go through. The burdens I carry are light when I release them to the Lord, but if I don't release them, they will be mine to carry without help. I must release my burdens to Him, not to have them taken away, but to have the grace to walk with them or walk out of them. No one but God knows the battles and burdens each of us deal with every day. Only God knows how I struggle to stay within my limits, how I have this burning desire in me every day to help others while being stuck in what sometimes seems like a prison.

I know that God is teaching me that praying, worshipping, and praising right here where I am touches Heaven and bounces right back down on those who need it. There are miracles happening in this place that I won't know about until I get to Heaven. This truth helps me keep my eyes on things of eternal significance. This is where I can attain and keep my joy, resting in God and knowing that I have a destiny of eternal value. If you count the cost and receive a new revelation, your understanding expands, and you realize that you have already started walking in that revealed knowledge because you stepped out in faith and now it's a lot easier to continue because you understand more pieces of the puzzle. That's how faith works.

Unfortunately, some people stop short of walking out their revelation by failing to do something with it; they stop there and don't move forward. You may even try to go back the way you came, but once you pass through a season of time, you cannot go back or retrace those steps. When you try to go back, you take another route, and if it's not the path the Lord has prepared, you'll be in trouble. The reason we get revelation in the first place is because God deems us able to receive it. We may have asked for help, so when God gives us that piece of revelation, we're responsible for moving with it, and that doesn't involve moving backwards or settling where we are.

Finding out I would be doing the exercises for the rest of my life did not bring me fuzzy warm feelings, but I feel good when I'm consistent in doing them. On the other hand, I get excited when I realize that as I praise, worship, and pray I greatly affect the kingdom. Understanding my part helped to dissolve some of the discontentment I was feeling all the time.

Paul and Silas praised and prayed in jail after being beaten, and God sent an earthquake. Their jailer and his whole household believed in Jesus and got baptized (Acts 16:25–34). Don't ever think that those everyday routine things that you've taken responsibility for and have consistently done your part in don't count in the kingdom. God honours those acts of obedience. They are important to Him, so they should be important to us. God sees everything and cares so much for us. He wants to spend all day and night with us, and if you still your heart and stop and listen, you can feel Him right there, because He never leaves. His presence surrounds us; it is the very air we breathe. As we keep walking along the path with Him, in thankfulness and gratitude for what He has done and is doing in our lives, He keeps releasing revelation so that we can take one more step with confidence that He is there!

GOING DEEPER

REFLECTION

1. Are there areas in your life where you are not consistent? Do you know why?

2. Is there revelation you have received that you have not put into action? If the answer is yes, what is holding you back?

3. Do you feel what you do has no effect on the Kingdom of God? Ask Holy Spirit to show you the eternal value of consistently doing what you know to do.

DECREE

Let the peace of Christ keep you in tune with each other, in step with each other. None of this going off and doing your own thing. And cultivate thankfulness. Let the Word of Christ—the Message—have the run of the house. Give it plenty of room in your lives. Instruct and direct one another using good common sense. And sing, sing your hearts out to God! Let every detail in your lives—words, actions, whatever—be done in the name of the Master, Jesus, thanking God the Father every step of the way. (Colossian 3:17, MSG) So let's not get tired of doing what is good. At just the right time we will reap a harvest of blessing if we don't give up. (Galatian 6:9) With all this going for us, my dear, dear friends, stand your ground. And don't hold back. Throw yourselves into the work of the Master, confident that nothing you do for him is a waste of time or effort. (1 Corinthians 15:58, MSG)

PRAYER

Thank you, Father, for making me in Your image. Thank You for not giving up on me when I gave up on myself. I choose to pick up my cross and follow

Holy Spirit along the path You have for me. I choose to move forward towards those battles You have for me. I repent for being a hearer of the Word but not a doer. I pray You will give me revelation of what You would have me do and how that will affect my world for the Kingdom of God. In Jesus' name. Amen.

FURTHER READING

James 1

Matthew 11:28–30

Driven by Eternity, John Bevere Ministries Inc., Warner Faith, 2006

CHAPTER TWENTY

BREAKTHROUGH

Things got intense after Christmas. We were meeting with bankers and financial advisors and gathering information so we could make an informed decision regarding our business. I began to notice how my emotions were affecting my body. I'd come a long way in recognizing my emotions and getting myself to stay calm so that my brain would start sending the right signals to relax my muscles. Now I was learning to take it one step further to process external stress in a way that didn't upset my physical body and throw the muscles into a state of disarray.

I was learning how to separate my emotions from my physical body and to deal in a calm and relaxed way with other people's emotions. Awesome! It's a process, and it makes me think back to when I was a dental assistant. I had to learn to disassociate some of the procedures we were doing from what I actually saw and who we were doing them on, so I already had some practice at separating my emotions. In this process I will be quick to listen and slow to speak, and that will help me to continue to see from the eternal perspective so my emotions will not overtake me.

I also started the new ball system to stimulate the fascia that envelops the whole body. They were very simple exercises, and I immediately felt different when I was done, even after the first time. Best of all, they did *not* cause any pain; in fact, they made my jaw feel like it actually belonged in my body. My skin felt alive. I don't recall my skin ever feeling that way before. I felt like I was standing firmer on the ground. I'd recommend them to anyone. I probably felt this difference more intensely than others might because I'd been in training for several years to assess and be aware of my body. If you'd asked me before my accident if I would ever do this kind of thing, I would have laughed. I'm a different person now. I'm more flexible. I broke out of the closet of confinement into a whole new world of possibilities, even while living with physical limitations. I never thought I could be content in the waiting. I am more whole now than I ever dreamed I could be when I started my walk with God.

Time moved on and the balls became part of my routine of loosening, stretching, and strengthening to keep me in the momentum of forward movement. The long, cold winter didn't seem that long to me. I had lots to do, and it didn't seem like I ever had enough time to get everything done. I was sticking to the schedule I made up every morning, but also allowing myself to be flexible to anything that might come up. Not much interrupted my day, and routine set in. I continued doing meditation exercises and felt very rested and at peace. I practiced positioning myself to relax, and I could rest. That is an amazing victory for a person who couldn't content herself to sit for any length of time for the better part of fifty years without thinking of something she could be doing. It's true ... nothing is impossible with God.

I started noticing that the muscles in my arms were feeling pulled and they ached most of the time whenever I did anything with them. Discouragement tried to rear its ugly head and kept whispering, "If it isn't one thing, it's another. Is this ever going to end?"

Have you ever heard those defeating words? They are not your thoughts. We have an enemy, and he likes to place thoughts in our heads that we think are ours, but they're not. I encouraged myself by speaking the truth. I wasn't going to go back there. I was moving forward. My jaw was feeling better, so other little hurts that were already there were going to surface. I was aiming for wholeness, but I wasn't whole yet. I remembered that I'd experienced issues with my arms before. I had an appointment with Joy coming up in the near future, and she would have answers for what my body was doing.

While I was waiting for my appointment date, I managed to catch a bad cold, which doesn't happen very often to me. The pain was the most horrible sinus pain I'd ever experienced, and it made my jaw ache. Coughing made my head and back hurt. I'd forgotten how painful a simple cold can be when you have a sensitive head and jaw. I'm learning every day that there's nothing ordinary about me. I am extraordinary, one of a kind, an original masterpiece. I took a quick trip to my doctor—who I know must have missed seeing me since it had been a while—got a prescription to get rid of the nasty infection, and went home. I knew this cold had an expected end, so it didn't do much to set me back. It made me realize that I could catch something common every now and again.

I woke up one morning and, suddenly, this masterpiece of God started experiencing swelling in my cheeks. I felt like one of the three chipmunks—Alvin. Well, maybe more like Simon, or perhaps Theodore ... he looked like he had the biggest cheeks. I had to be careful not to bite my cheeks when I shut my mouth, and eating was an adventure. I had no pain, just this odd swelling on both sides of my head. I really liked the fact that I had no pain, although it felt weird. I contacted Joy to see if she had any experience with this type of thing. She assured me it wasn't a normal occurrence in the course of treatment. The swelling mysteriously left after a couple of days. I found out later that it was connected with my lymphatic system.

Right before my next appointment with Joy, I noticed that I could now hold my head aligned to my shoulders. It just happened. It's like I could picture the plumb line I could align myself to so I could stand straight. I was aligned when my head moved from being tilted slightly to the right to the straight spot. Now my brain understood it and I could do it. Holding a head that weighs at least ten pounds back about an inch farther than it's used to is a lot of work, but I would succeed. Victory!

This was such wonderful news, because when I was aligned my jaw didn't hurt and my shoulders didn't ache. My back didn't get sore, because I was standing in the proper position. Oh, the joy! Oh, the peace! Now I needed to practice every day to stay in the proper alignment for as long as I could. I had progressed to this point and gained this much land—I would not stop the forward momentum. I was taking all the land that was mine with wisdom and patient endurance. I am confident the whole land of my body will be mine one day.

I went for my appointment with Joy as scheduled. The good news of my alignment was well received, and she was happy for me. I told her about my sore arms, especially the left one. It was very sore after the accident, and for a long time I couldn't cross it over my body without a lot of pain. I figured now was the time to get it in the correct position.

I lay on the table, and Joy did a workout on me. She had her leg up on the table so she could apply more pressure. Apparently, as my left arm was pulled towards my head, and the fascia was pulled tight in my chest, there was no flow in that area. My right arm wasn't as tight, so she loosened my right chest area quickly. My right arm didn't respond as well as my left arm. When I asked her if it was resisting, she said no. My right arm just didn't know what to do, because my brain had kept it in this holding pattern for so long to protect it. In my words, my arm didn't know how to be free!

My brain needed to let go of the old and embrace the new. I started doing some arm releases that I'd done previously, and also some footloose and fancy free arm swinging. I felt like a little girl in a green pasture, swinging my arms around with the wind beneath my wings! Joy said I was very good at getting my body to relax in order to do these exercises, which was a real compliment. If you could have seen me six months ago, telling my body to "relax and let go," you'd know exactly what I had achieved. Look what the Lord has done!

DEEP FREEDOM AND MENTORSHIP

> Mentor: someone who teaches or gives help and advice to a less experienced and often younger person.
>
> Deep:
> 1. going far inward from the outside or the front edge of something;
> 2. located far inside something.

You may be wondering why I would put mentorship in this section when we're talking about breakthrough. In order to get to the level of freedom we all want, we must go through a process. There are no shortcuts, and we cannot get there alone. We must trust someone with our deepest struggles in order to come to that place where we see clearly and know what we must do to keep moving forward.

Within our family structure (church or blood family) there are levels of relationship. We don't relate to everyone the same, but each one of those connections are important, because together we make the whole of what God intended for us individually and corporately. It's called interdependence, and that's how a family works together for the greater good.

When you ask Jesus into your heart, you enter into the family of God and embrace the truth that you are a son or daughter of the Most High God. The purpose of our journey here on earth is to learn to walk like children of God. To do that, we need the help of those who have gone before us, those spiritual mothers and fathers that God has placed in our lives. They are our mentors—the ones who have paid the price and have attained wisdom to pass along to us.

Jesus set the example with the twelve disciples. He asked them to "follow," and they did. If you don't know the rest of the story, it's all recorded in the New Testament for your reading pleasure. We all need spiritual fathers and mothers (mentors) to learn from in order to grow and mature in the ways of the kingdom. Mentoring represents the highest level of trust most of us will probably have with another person. We can tell how much we trust God by how much we trust those mentors in our lives ... how real we are with them. That's the kingdom way. God wants us to trust those He has placed in authority over us to prove that when we say we trust Him, we have in fact faced the reality of a situation with someone who can tell us whether or not we are actually trusting God. We need help to get out from under deception. Deep inside we all want to trust God.

Mentors help us make the transition from thinking we are trusting God to actually doing the action of trusting Him. When we get the breakthrough we're waiting for, we are responsible for following through and walking out that freedom. Sometimes I didn't know how to respond when I recognized that I'd responded in an ungodly way. Without help from my mentor, I could easily have gone back to the same responses and, unfortunately, the same results. My mentor and I have had some amazing revelations—revelations God only gave me in part, and the fullness was released when we got together. Scripture does say that where two or more are gathered in His name, He is there (Matthew 18:20). Once we got the full revelation, Pastor C. helped me to practically apply what we'd discovered.

Life before community was dull and gray. Getting together with others of a like mind is so important. My church family and my blood family have become treasures to me. In order to have the relationships with others we all long for, we must get connected with people. Real relationships can be fulfilling and give us the encouragement to push forward when life gets tough—because it gets tough for everyone at some point. Having those ones around you to lift you up, rejoice with you in the happy times, and cry with you in the not-so-happy times is the precious gift of community. God has true friends for you who are not afraid to tell you the truth, because they love you.

I have learned that I can co-operate with others, whether I am delegating and leading or getting under and supporting someone else who is leading. Coming from a place of control ruled by fear, it has taken me a little while to understand that I am just as capable of leading as I am of supporting others. I have security in the fact that God has my back. He is in control, and that is such a comfort to me. It takes some time to get to that place of confidence, and family plus mentorship is how you get there. Being interdependent takes practice, and it's a very humbling experience sometimes, but iron sharpens iron (Proverbs 27:17) ... and who doesn't want to be sharp?

As we learn to live as sons and daughters, we will eventually be the baby bird that learned to fly, and we'll soar with God to greater heights. We don't do all that flying alone—our family is right there with us, each one helping the other, moving forward and soaring higher together as the body of Christ advancing the Kingdom of God.

That's the way God set up the kingdom to function; it's His order, and He sent Jesus to show us how it's done. If it worked for the disciples who walked the earth with Him, it will work for us as His disciples who walk with Holy Spirit today. God has someone He wants you to learn from, to sit at their feet, so-to-speak. Don't miss the opportunity to soar higher than you can imagine. Ask Holy Spirit who He has for you. Who has He set aside to pour into you so you can be all you were destined to be as a child of God? Mentors help us go deeper into the depths of God, which are limitless and go on from this life into eternity.

GOING DEEPER

REFLECTION

1. Do you have a mentor or a mature believer with whom you can be vulnerable?

2. If not, can you identify why you haven't made that commitment?

3. Are you being transparent with those God has placed in your life to guide you?

DECREE

Jesus, undeterred, went right ahead and gave his charge: "God authorized and commanded me to commission you: Go out and train everyone you meet, far and near, in this way of life, marking them by baptism in the threefold name: Father, Son, and Holy Spirit. Then instruct them in the practice of all I have commanded you. I'll be with you as you do this, day after day after day, right up to the end of the age." (Matthew 28:19–20, MSG) My response is to get down on my knees before the Father, this magnificent Father who parcels out all heaven and earth. I ask him to strengthen you by his Spirit—not a brute strength but a glorious inner strength—that Christ will live in you as you open the door and invite him in. And I ask him that with both feet planted firmly on love, you'll be able to take in with all followers of Jesus the extravagant dimensions of Christ's love. Reach out and experience the breadth! Test its length! Plumb the depths! Rise to the heights! Live full lives, full in the fullness of God. (Ephesians 3:14–19, MSG) Instruct the wise, and they will be even wiser. Teach the righteous, and they will learn even more. (Proverbs 9:9) Fear of the Lord is the foundation of true knowledge, but fools despise wisdom and discipline. (Proverbs 1:7)

PRAYER

Jesus, You have shown me the way to kingdom living, and I want to follow You. Help me to be real so I can follow You to the highest place You have for me. I want to learn to soar higher and higher with You above the clouds so I can see with Your eyes. I pray You would equip the mentor You have for me. Help me to know You more by getting to know who I am in You. Amen.

FURTHER READING

Psalm 127

1 Kings 19:19–21

2 Kings 2:1–15

CHAPTER TWENTY-ONE

FOCUS IS EVERYTHING

With my head now in alignment, I noticed that when I did my floor exercises, I had switched to focusing on how I was holding my body instead of the exercise. What a difference in my routine! I began focusing on my core strength and my position instead of what I was doing. I was also learning to stand in my faith to believe and on the freedom I'd attained, and to move and live and have my being from that position. I was learning not to strive, but instead to follow the leading of the Spirit within me. What a release of joy! I no longer had to fight with myself to do what I knew to do. I had peace when I rested and peace when I moved. It was a place in which I would grow, and I was looking forward to doing that in the days, months and years ahead.

The sixth anniversary of my accident came and went with out incident. I thanked God I was still here and was becoming more fully alive daily with Him at my side. I still had chronic pain, but God always provided a way out. More often than not, I took the way out instead of remaining stubborn and in pain. Change takes a lifetime, and I was ready for the long haul of learning about me and what I was capable of.

I also celebrated my fifty-fifth birthday that year and grabbed hold of the freedom that fifty-five brought. The number five means grace in Hebrew, and I believe I had a double portion of grace that year to do all that God had in His plan for me. Six years ago God said, "Come away with me, Carol," and I replied, "I am coming." The rest is His story of my life as I continue to follow along the path He has set before me.

That summer I received good news. During an appointment with Joy, she did her usual head analysis and was putting me into the proper position when she said my head felt more normal than some heads she treats that hadn't been in a major car accident. Woo hoo! This announcement meant I was graduating! My appointments were stretched farther apart, and we aimed at complete freedom from therapy away from my home. She said I was 99 per cent perfect, and I believed it! Walking with the Lord and following the Shepherd's leading had made me whole. It looked different than I might have thought at first, but I received the perfection of being me. With the blood of Jesus covering me, I am perfect in my Father's eyes. And it's not just for a select few. The perfection of being you is available ... just believe.

FOCUS

> Focus: a state or condition permitting clear perception or understanding of a point of concentration.

Focus is important. What you focus on determines where you will go. When we keep our focus on the circumstances of our lives instead of the victory Jesus has already won for us at the cross, we won't have the peace or joy to which we are entitled. We'll feel abandoned and hopeless, waiting with dread for the next circumstance to come. That doesn't sound like a very nice way to live, but the truth will set you free! God's Word tells us to focus and meditate on what is good and right. When we do this, we can be thankful. Nothing moves you forward like gratitude for what you have instead of wanting what you don't have.

I was doing what I knew to do and I wanted change in my life, but I couldn't see anything happening. I had breakthrough after breakthrough, and then for what seemed like forever, I felt that nothing was changing. I was assured by my mentor that I wasn't doing anything "wrong," which was something I struggled with. As I've grown and matured, I've learned to cast wrong thoughts down and not agree with them. I am a child of God, and Holy Spirit will convict me when I do something wrong. As I continue, that wrong pattern of thinking is changing. It's amazing how the renewing of our minds happens daily with every wrong thought we catch and replace with what God says about us. It builds our faith and trust when we realize that we don't think that way anymore.

God is after our trust. He wants us to believe He is a good Father and that He knows what's best for us. When we think He has abandoned us, He wants to show us that He's right there with us. We need to re-adjust our focus back to Him in order to know that He is there and He really does care for us.

When change doesn't happen as quickly as I think it should, I can easily change my focus to hungering for change instead of hungering for more of Jesus. It's a subtle shift, but staying in the right position definitely gets you to the right place in God's right timing.

God has given us five natural senses: sight, hearing, smell, touch, and taste. Just as we use our senses to experience this world, God wants us to use our senses to experience Him and the supernatural world. This is part of maturing and growing as we move forward. God doesn't want us to become familiar with only one or two ways He communicates with us. He wants us to experience the full measure of who He is. He wants to teach us how to connect and relate to Him with all of our senses.

Just as we enjoy a beautiful sunset while listening to the sounds of the waves on the shore, smelling the freshness of the air, touching the sand between our toes, and tasting some delectable treat all at the same time, God wants us to experience that with our senses in the supernatural world. Our spiritual senses unlock when we open our hearts, trust God, and spend time with Him so we can learn more about Him and how to function as His children. This is the supernatural lifestyle we live as children of God. We open new mysteries every day by reading His Word, hearing His voice, breathing Him in, seeing what He sees, feeling His presence surround us, and actually tasting and drinking of Him. The Bible does say taste and see that the Lord is good (Psalm 34:8). This is the fullness of God, the love of the Father experienced in all the ways human beings can experience Him.

The depths of His love are unfathomable. We can get into His presence and feel like we have soaked up all the love we need for a lifetime, and still there is more. His love is never-ending and far-reaching.

Once we receive our Father's love, we're ready to go out and love the ones God has placed in our world. This is the Kingdom of God in action; we are the hands and feet of Jesus, bringing the Father's love to a lost and dying world. Then back we go into His presence to be filled up with more of His love to go out and give away. What a wonderful God cycle to be part of! Jesus is the bridge to that love. When we ask Jesus into our hearts, we cross over and experience the Father's love over and over again. It's not a one-time crossing. The grace of Jesus is there for you, so take that step of faith and experience God. The possibilities are limitless and priceless!

GOING DEEPER

REFLECTION

1. What holds you back from experiencing God to the fullest? What stops you from crossing the bridge in front of you?

2. Do you know you can continually cross that bridge and encounter the Father's love over and over again?

3. Is there an area in your heart where you are afraid to let in the Father's love? He knows what's in there anyway. Ask Holy Spirit to come in and heal your heart and fill it up with love.

DECREE

Always be full of joy in the Lord. I say it again—rejoice! Let everyone see that you are considerate in all you do. Remember, the Lord is coming soon. Don't worry about anything; instead, pray about everything. Tell God what you need, and thank him for all he has done. Then you will experience God's peace, which exceeds anything we can understand. His peace will guard your hearts and minds as you live in Christ Jesus. And now, dear brothers and sisters, one final thing. Fix your thoughts on what is true, and honorable, and right, and pure, and lovely, and admirable. Think about things that are excellent and worthy of praise. Keep putting into practice all you learned and received from me—everything you heard from me and saw me doing. Then the God of peace will be with you. (Philippians 4:4–9) Jesus told him, "I am the way, the truth, and the life. No one can come to the Father except through me." (John 14:6) He personally carried our sins in his body on the cross so that we can be dead to sin and live for what is right. By his wounds you are healed. (1 Peter 2:24)

PRAYER

Father, I don't want to miss anything you have for me. I ask for forgiveness for believing the lie that this is all there is. I break any agreement I've made with the enemy that keeps me away from receiving more of Your love. I cross over the bridge that the cross of Jesus has made for me, and I am ready to receive the love that I have resisted. I will focus on Jesus, and the cares of this world will fade away. I thank you, Jesus, for the cross that made a way to the Father for me. Amen.

FURTHER READING

Philippians 2:14–15

Hebrews 13

God is Good by Bill Johnson, Destiny Image Publishers Inc., 2016

CHAPTER TWENTY-TWO

I THOUGHT I WAS HEALED

The five-year anniversary of coming out of denial and actually starting the process of discovering me came in the middle of 2014. I thought I'd let go of any expectations of what wholeness and healing would look like for me, but I discovered I was wrong. Deep inside I had a wrong mindset of what it meant when I was told, "You are aligned; you are healed." I believed it, but my actions proved that my heart wasn't convinced of what healing looked like for me.

One day I was outside attempting a light pruning of some bushes in the back yard. We have two hundred-foot high evergreen trees with branches to the ground. The previous winter had been hard on the lower branches, and I saw that one of them didn't look very well. I left the bushes I was trimming and cut the sick-looking evergreen branch off. I took a look at my tree and saw there was a big hole where the branch had been.

My next intelligent thought occurred when I stepped back forty-five minutes later and saw what I had done. The two trees were now trimmed up five feet from the ground, with bare branches poking out all around. They looked like carousels with poles sticking out, but no little animals on the ends of them. I felt sick and was in extreme pain. I braced some of the bigger branches on my knee and used my body as a type of wedge to cut them. Can you picture that? For someone who was supposed to be doing minimal physical labour, this was insane. I thought of one word to describe what had happened to me. I was "driven."

My mind then went into over-drive. I'd made a huge mess, and I was going to have to figure out how to clean it up. I needed a chainsaw to cut down the carousel poles, but sanity had returned and I knew I didn't have the strength to start our chainsaw. Thank God for His mercy. My husband, Dave, was busy at our continuing business adventure, so I decided to call our neighbour and ask if he could come and cut down the branches. He must have thought I was crazy. He couldn't come until the next day. That was going to be too late for me, because Dave and my daughters would be home in a couple of hours to see what I had done. What was a girl to do? If I didn't have this mess cleaned up, I'd be in big trouble. It turned out I could do nothing but wait until someone came home. There were branches everywhere, and I didn't have any energy left to do anything but take a couple of pills and lie down. I asked God to please forgive me and help me, because I didn't know what to do. What a mess.

When everyone came home I confessed what I'd done and asked for help. Not all of my lessons of the past several years had been in vain. It was the weekend, and the next day Dave stayed home to help. My daughters agreed to help too. He cut off the branches I couldn't, and the girls helped clean up some of the tree parts scattered over the ground. They weren't very happy, because I'd made a big mess and now they had to help clean it up. On top of everything, I'd injured my body, and I was very sore, but I said nothing about the pain. Would you? This was no laughing matter, but when I told others what I'd done, they laughed a lot and I felt even worse. I didn't know why I'd done that to myself, so how could I explain it to anyone else? I told everyone I was "driven" to cut the branches, even though I knew not to do it. I took one step and then something in me took over.

I had an appointment with Joy the following week, which meant I didn't have to wait too long before this Humpty Dumpty could be put back together again. I took a friend with me, and she was very quick to let Joy know I had something of significance to confess to her. Oh, the shame of having to tell everyone what I had done and to see that look of shock on their faces! She worked on me and did what had to be done, and it was a very painful appointment—physically and emotionally. I'm sure my spirit was grieved too. She told me I adjusted back to an aligned position fairly well, but I barely heard her through the nausea and dizziness I was feeling.

"So much for being healed," I said to myself.

I thought I could do what I used to do. I was healed, wasn't I? This smarty pants hadn't quite arrived yet, and it was agreed by the three of us—Joy, my friend, and I—that the next time I wanted to trim trees, I'd hire someone. It would be less expensive and hurtful than an appointment with a craniosacral therapist.

PRIDE

> Pride: an insolent and empty assurance which trusts in its own power and resources and shamefully despises and violates divine laws and human rights. (Strong's Concordance, G212)

Pride is sin, and it's something we all deal with in life. It can drive us to build a high tower for ourselves, only to push us off the top, sometimes wounding us critically. It was a very humbling experience for me when I came out of my stupor and realized what I had done in what is now referred to as my "tree cutting incident." I knew my boundaries; I knew what to do or not to do, but I did it anyway. I know now that something inside of me pushed me and wanted me to hurt myself in order to get me out of the agreement with God I'd made to keep me safe.

When Joy told me that I was aligned and had graduated, I still had a remnant of that old pattern of thinking that I was going to be able to do what I could before the car accident. Then pride took over. I was shocked when I came to my senses and saw what I was capable of doing when I stepped out of the will of God. It scared me, embarrassed me, and shamed me. Sin makes you stupid. While I was in my cutting frenzy, I do remember hearing, "Will you stop now?" I ignored that still, calm voice of wisdom, just in case you were wondering if Holy Spirit had abandoned me. He was there asking me to stop, speaking sense into my senselessness. He will not force us; we must choose for ourselves what we're going to do and the path we'll take. I chose the crooked path this time, but I did learn a valuable lesson. I need Holy Spirit every day, all day long, everywhere my feet tread, because satan and my flesh are right there waiting to lead me into trouble ... into sin. Sin makes you do stupid things.

My sin not only affected me, but those in my world. That's what our sin does—it has a domino effect. My husband lost valuable time at work. My daughters changed their plans to help clean up my mess. I had also done damage to my physical body, which could be called abuse, from Joy's point of view.

I did what I knew to do and repented. I asked God to forgive me, and I also told my family I was sorry. The remnant of that old pattern of thinking was going to move out. I am determined to keep humbling myself before God and others, because pride will not rule me. As I continue to honour others above myself, pride has to head towards the door and out of my life. Pride will push you into doing what you know not to do. Its voice is familiar, because we've heard it throughout our lives. It's so deep in our sub-conscious, we have conversations with it and sometimes mistake it for Holy Spirit because it sounds good, is convincing, and pleases our flesh. We will face pride until we die. It takes many forms and is rooted in selfishness. It does not consider others and sets itself up against the ways of God.

I learned early in my walk with Jesus that satan was the head angel in charge of worship in Heaven who thought it would be cool to be like God and rule. He is the ultimate creature of pride and arrogance. I can't help but think that the pride of satan and the worshipping of God are connected. If satan was the head worshipper and was thrown out of Heaven for planning a mutiny against God, then wouldn't it stand to reason that he would attempt to do the same in this world? Satan cannot create anything, but he's very good at twisting things around, like he did in the Garden of Eden. God had created something to be beautiful, but satan twisted it into something he could use to kill, steal, and destroy.

I am a worshipper. Music has played a big role in my life, and I listen to it all the time. It fills your spirit and lifts your soul. When I started listening to Holy Spirit-inspired music, it was like nothing I'd ever experienced. When I sang along it went straight to my heart. I was praising God by singing, and it changed the atmosphere around me. It's wonderful to experience God in the music He has sent from Heaven.

Praise is one thing, but worship is quite another. When you take control of your attitude and sing praises, you can enter into worshipping God for who He is and what He has done for us. Worship leads you to a place of obedience to God's Word, hearing that still, small voice of Holy Spirit taking you from where you are to a better place where you can see things from God's perspective. The Bible says the highest form of worship is obedience. Worship gets you to that place where you want to obey and follow God, because you know He has the best for you. We don't worship God because He needs it. We worship God because we need Him, and He can't stay away from His kids when they praise and worship Him. It's a win-win situation.

Satan hates it when we obey God, because that's worship. He uses pride to get us into a place of disobedience so that the best the Father has for us is either held up or squashed. First comes pride, then the crash—the bigger the ego, the harder the fall (Proverbs 16:18). God doesn't want us to fall! When we stay within our boundaries and follow Holy Spirit, we still have some ups and downs, but we can be assured that God will lift us up to see from His perspective. And pride will be under our feet ... right where it belongs.

GOING DEEPER

REFLECTION

1. Are there areas in your life where you know the right thing to do but you don't do it?

2. The Bible tells us to examine and guard our hearts against the temptation of satan. Are there areas in your heart where you have let your guard down? Where are you tempted?

3. Ask Holy Spirit to heal those areas and release strategy to move forward.

DECREE

You rescue the humble, but you humiliate the proud. You light a lamp for me. The Lord, my God, lights up my darkness. In your strength I can crush an army; with my God I can scale any wall. (Psalm 18:27–29) Hallelujah! Sing to God a brand-new song, praise him in the company of all who love him. Let all Israel celebrate their Sovereign Creator, Zion's children exult in their King. Let them praise his name in dance; strike up the band and make great music! And why? Because God delights in his people, festoons plain folk with salvation garlands! (Psalm 149:1–4, MSG) The Lord is good and does what is right; he shows the proper path to those who go astray. (Psalm 25:8)

PRAYER

Jesus, I want to walk humbly before You and do what is right in Your eyes. I repent of pride. Forgive me. Teach me how to worship You in spirit and truth. Show me the straight path You have for me. My body is the Temple of God, and I want to steward this body for Your glory. Amen.

FURTHER READING

Isaiah 14:12–21

Philippians 2:5–8

1 Peter 5:5–11

Humility and Absolute Surrender by Andrew Murray, Hendrickson Publishers, Inc., 2005

Pride Versus Humility by Derek Prince, Whitaker House, 2016

CHAPTER TWENTY-THREE

EXPANDING BOUNDARIES

Joy put my head back together, and I thought I was behaving myself very well by staying within the boundaries I was working with during this season. Boundaries change constantly, because there is a season for everything. I was in pain, and it seemed to be more constant than I was used to. I was also angry, and I began to see it seeping into everything and at everyone. I had a tone in my voice when I was in pain, and it was getting worse as my pain levels began soaring to a higher level than they had for a long time. The more I hurt, the angrier I felt. The tree-cutting incident may have been behind me, but there was something ugly coming to the surface, and it made me mad.

I started experiencing extreme pain in my right arm, and upon visiting my doctor I discovered I had tendonitis, a repercussion from cutting the trees. On the outside it may have appeared that I was handling with grace the fact that I had to wear a tension gadget on my arm and cut back on physical work again. Inside, however, I was hopping mad, and that undealt-with anger got worse and worse.

My next visit with Joy in the fall revealed a lot. I went to this appointment desperate for something to help, and I had given up fighting. I was at my breaking point. I asked her flat out what I needed to do to keep away from pain as much as possible.

She gave me a list of dos and don'ts to help me walk within my boundaries. I posted them in a few places and did my best to stick with the Post-It Plan. It helped considerably, and I felt I was gaining ground for the first time in a couple of months. The anger subsided to a simmering boil, and it remained on the back burner for the time being.

I was still experiencing headaches that Joy attributed to my tight jaw. My left side was causing the bones to pull to the left and this, in turn, made the right side of my neck hurt. I learned that muscles move bones! She showed me how to stretch my jaw muscles from above, which was a new, painful experience. My back was also extremely sore, and she said it had just been hiding behind other things and was now making itself known. This sounded exactly like what I was experiencing with the anger I was feeling. I felt like I was in a "limbo" state where nothing was happening. I was supposed to be aligned and healed, and here I was angry and in pain. All this was just part of the remnants of the injury; it was the leftovers. I don't like leftovers very much.

The jaw-stretching exercises made me cry for the first ten days, but I did them anyway. At Joy's suggestion, I tried walking to help with the back issue. My body didn't like the cold at all, so I stopped walking outside and starting walking on the spot … marching like a soldier. Just a reminder here that God always gives us a way out of our pain. We must choose to take it.

A couple of months went by with routine setting in, and I seemed to be managing okay. The anger had not completely left, and it spewed out of my mouth in the most unpleasant ways. Because I could see it, it seemed to make me angrier. I did my best to use self-discipline and keep moving forward.

Christmas is a busy time for everyone, and our household was no different—decorations to put up, presents to purchase and wrap, and functions to attend. For those who suffer from chronic pain, it's a very trying time to balance all the extra things and still maintain a schedule beneficial to one's sanity.

The anger that simmered on the back burner moved to the front burner, which must have been turned on high. I was determined to find out where this was coming from and what could be done. An appointment with Pastor C. proved to be what was needed. I told her how I was feeling and that I was angry all the time. I needed help, because I could see this anger every time it came out, and it had been coming out for two months now. Even though I was apologizing and telling my family I wasn't angry at them in particular, I couldn't seem to stop, and I was starting to dislike myself very much.

"You should consider writing down your pain levels morning, noon, and night," she said, "and posting them somewhere on your fridge so your family knows your pain level." She told me I hold pain well until it gets to a point that I can't take it anymore, and when I reach that breaking point, it comes out in every direction.

I looked at her and started crying. I didn't want to do it. This seemed like very odd behaviour for me. It was a good plan, and it would show my family when I needed help and when not to ask for my help. I didn't understand my distress at all. I finally agreed to do it, but I didn't want to and didn't see how this was going to help my anger. But God knew what it was going to do, and it turned out well.

I went home and told my family about it. They were ecstatic; they thought it was a great idea. I wasn't on board, but I found out a little later that I was still dealing with this pride issue.

After the first couple of days, charting my pain got easier, although the pain didn't let up. I did find the anger subsided a bit, and I didn't see the world through its red cloud. My next appointment with Pastor C. was very revealing. We discovered that I had all this anger because pride had told me that I had to do this walk by myself. I went to all of my appointments and treatments by myself. I thought I had to deal with my life in this state of pain by myself, even though I didn't want to. When I began charting my pain levels, I chose to let my family in to help me, which meant humbling myself before God. I repented of pride, and the charting was a breeze. Even though I was angry, my obedience gave Holy Spirit access to come in and separate my emotions from my pain. I began to experience healing in my emotions, and my physical body responded by settling down and relaxing.

I started to see glimpses of why I was angry, which allowed me to talk to God and ask Him why. He told me that He wanted me healed, but I was resisting what He'd called me to do. I was fighting against it, even though I didn't know what it all entailed. I repented, and the pain faded away. I felt like the Carol I had come to know and love.

God had a good plan for me, and it wasn't going to change just because I had a car accident. By trusting Him, I can face each day head on. I'm letting Jesus go before me to lead me into the adventure and opportunity He has for me today and all the days to come.

ANGER

> Anger: a strong feeling of being upset or annoyed because of some thing wrong or bad; the feeling that makes someone want to hurt other people, to shout, etc.

I lived most of my life either being angry or happy. As I got older, I seemed to be more angry than happy. Throughout this journey, I discovered that anger is a secondary emotion. God gave us emotions, and it's okay to feel them. Anger is a caution—a "Wait a minute, what's going on here?"—type of emotion. Anger speaks of a deeper issue, something that is not agreeable to us. We all experience anger, but the problem arises when we don't know what to do with our anger.

When I get angry, I can only hold it in for so long before it spews out everywhere, hurting everyone in its path. I've enjoyed a considerable amount of freedom from anger, and thought I'd learned how to deal with it. I'd made remarkable progress, but it seemed to come like a wave, trying to get me to lose my balance and make me walk a little slanted, a little crooked.

I asked God why I was so angry, and He showed me that I wanted things my way. That was unacceptable to me at that time, so I ignored that answer. I was already dealing with pride, which always wants its own way, but I didn't make that connection. Had I dug deeper with Holy Spirit, I could have avoided unnecessary pain.

There are things that always try to hold us back from the destiny God has for us. The enemy is after our destiny, because each of our destinies are important to the advancement of the

Kingdom of God. When we walk in time with God towards our destiny, we present a threat to the kingdom of darkness, so satan will try to take us off the course and out of the timing God has for us. When we do our part and ask God questions and respond to His answers, we move closer to what He wants us to accomplish. Then we can feel the fulfillment of a job well done. We all want to know why we are here and what our purpose is in life. We're all searching for significance. When we meet with God and learn more of His character, we are able to trust that He has a good plan for us.

As I continue along the path of my destiny, I see life in a greater depth. I see into the natural world with more precision, and God begins to uncover the fullness of His love and who He is. You may already be living God's purpose for you, but there's always a greater depth to explore; however, this depth can be hidden by the cares of this world. We know there's more, but we don't know how to get there from here. God knows, and He wants us to get there. He wants us to enjoy life the kingdom way, where circumstances around us and our flesh don't dictate how we feel or act. I wanted to get out of the anger, but I really didn't want to do anything to get me to where I wanted to be. I was stuck.

Wrong cycles start when we get stuck and don't seek help from those God has placed in our lives as our spiritual authorities. I didn't want to go around the same mountain of anger again. Each time I dealt with that emotion, I came closer to keeping my authority over it, because I learned how to release it on different levels each time I asked for help. At the beginning of the process, I thought I'd done something wrong, because I was dealing with the same thing repeatedly. This is why those we have chosen to place in authority over us are so important. They can see things from the outside when we are on the inside—confused, frustrated, or, in my case, angry. I was dealing with anger on a much higher plane and at a much deeper level than I ever had before.

When Holy Spirit released the strategy of charting my pain levels and bringing them to the light, He could begin to separate that emotion from what was really going on. Then I could move out of the pride that was being held in place by anger. I began to see into the depths of pride like I had never before. The pride that said I had to do everything by myself and no one could help me was a liar. That lie was easily remedied—repent, ask for help, and become interdependent on others. That helps to build relationships, which is a priority for God.

Next I learned that I had expectations of myself that weren't fitting for a daughter of the King of kings and Lord of lords. I had an infection in my eye for a few months. I know now that was part of the twisted view I had of myself. That infection was coming out, and God was healing me of what I expected of myself—the pride of doing things perfectly instead of operating out of the excellence of God. He also showed me that because of the unrealistic expectations I'd placed on myself, I also had unrealistic expectations of others. I thought they should behave or respond a certain way, and when they didn't, I felt attacked. That made me angry, and I didn't know why. Jesus did say that we should get the log out of our own eye before we try to take the splinter out of someone else's eye (Matthew 7:5), and isn't that what we do? We get into other people's worlds and try to fix them before we examine ourselves and ask Holy Spirit to show us our spots and wrinkles. I'm not saying we cannot help others, but we must continue in the process, and we only have authority over what we overcome or are in the process of conquering.

The process of behaving like a son or daughter of God is a daily journey. As each new day begins, we have a new opportunity to advance the Kingdom of God, one step at a time. I'm glad there's no end to this process, because I'm fascinated by all God has done for me and all He has planned for me. I will not fear the future, because I know where I have come from. If He could do all that He's done for me in the ten short years I've walked with Him, I can hardly wait to see what the next ten years have in store! I have a confidence in God that can only come from trusting Him, and it allows me to view the world from His perspective. I never want to lose the wonder of the mystery of Christ in me.

We are here to choose. We can choose the tree of good and evil, or we can choose the tree of life. The tree of good and evil is the world's way; it's the wide road. Many will travel it and die. The tree of life is God's road; it's the narrow road, and few will choose it. Those were the trees in the Garden of Eden, and they are the same trees we choose between today. One leads to eternal life with God, and one leads to death ... an eternity spent in total separation from God.

Although we live in a fallen world, we see many of God's trademarks. The earth is God's, and we are here as His children to take it back! A world without God is a big, black hole—hell, actually, where satan and his angels are going. It wasn't created for people, and God doesn't want any human being to go there. But we each choose for ourselves. I choose Jesus. As I live and move and have my being in Him each day, I live a life of adventure and stand amazed at the God of wonder!

When we follow God, we constantly grow to contain more of Jesus and less of ourselves. Our circumstances are repurposed by God. Suffering is used for our benefit and the benefit of those in our world. It's like God's recycling—I overcome, and then I tell my testimony to help others overcome. This is my story, which is really His story of what He has done for me. Did you ever think recycling could be so much fun?

GOING DEEPER

REFLECTION

1. Ask Holy Spirit to reveal any areas where you have unrealistic expectations on yourself. Write them down.

2. Are there times you get angry and wonder why? Ask Holy Spirit to reveal the root cause of anger in your life.

3. Do you believe God has a plan and purpose for your life? Freedom allows us to step into the destiny God has for us. Are you moving forward in freedom?

DECREE

The hopes of the godly result in happiness, but the expectations of the wicked come to nothing. The way of the Lord is a stronghold to those with integrity, but it destroys the wicked. (Proverbs 10:28–29) "For I know the plans I have for you," says the Lord. "They are plans for good and not for disaster, to give you a future and a hope." (Jeremiah 29:11) "My thoughts are nothing like your thoughts," says the Lord. "And my ways are far beyond anything you could imagine. For just as the heavens are higher than the earth, so my ways are higher than your ways and my thoughts higher than your thoughts. (Isaiah 55:8–9) Let all that I am wait quietly before God, for my hope is in him. (Psalm 62:5)

PRAYER

Father, I put my expectations in You. I know You have a plan for my life, and I choose to follow You fully—spirit, soul, and body. I throw off all the cares of this world. I choose to focus on the Kingdom of God and push into all You have for me. I will not be denied the benefits of being a child of God, and I will align with You and set my sights on the prize of the high calling You have placed upon my life. Help me to accomplish all You have for me to do with this precious life you have given me. In Jesus' name I pray. Amen.

FURTHER READING

Matthew 5:21–22

Ephesians 4:26–27

Genesis 4:6–7

Keep Your Love on by Danny Silk, Red Arrow Media, 2013

CHAPTER TWENTY-FOUR

THE END OF THE BEGINNING

Our time together is at an end for now. It has been over seven years since my car accident, and I've decided to end here … although this is not the end by any stretch of the imagination. This, friend, is barely the beginning. I have learned so much in these years, more than I would have learned had I been working full-time, running here to there and back again, doing, doing, and doing some more. God wanted to spend quality time with me, so He asked me to come away and He set me apart. He didn't cause my car accident, but He used it to give me the best He had for me.

A friend of mine once told me that she saw me as a small lamb wrapped around a shepherd's neck. Apparently, this really happens when lambs damage their legs and cannot walk. The shepherd puts them around his neck so they will be safe while they heal. Think of how close that lamb is to the shepherd while around his neck, and how much it gets to know the characteristics of the shepherd. That lamb would never leave the shepherd, no matter what! This paints a wonderful picture of what Jesus has done with this once-broken and lost woman. A little while ago, I found something I'd written at the beginning of this journey, after coming out from under a great deal of depression. I was meant to find it so I could see how far I have come:

> Revelation to freedom. Dec 16/09—So it starts. I'm ready; the pain I've been holding since I was a young girl is a stumbling block, a wall that must come down so I can let God's love in. I am ready to let God into that pain so I can be healed. So much sorrow, so much anger, so much hurt. It was a loss of a life, really, as now I'm just a shell of a woman, like an eggshell surrounding the egg. The egg is me as a little girl and there I sit, waiting to be set free so I can just be how God intended me to be. The only one that can crack the egg and break the shell away is God, with my permission, of course. So I give you permission, God. Please break that hard shell that surrounds me, so I can be free to be me!

And here I am—free to be me. I have learned so much. I have had so many victories. If you knew me, you'd know all the hurt that God has taken away. All the pain from the car accident was a drop in the bucket compared to the hurts and wounds I had from life. All the physical symptoms that came out after that note was written were a picture of what was going on inside. God has truly healed me from the inside out. The shell is gone and the little girl is all grown up and living the life God intended for her.

I'm learning to schedule and adjust my life from my position of healing rather than learning to adjust to my pain. I am truly living without restrictions within the safe boundaries God has given me for my benefit, because I am worth keeping safe. I am His favourite. What else should I expect?

I'll leave you with my favourite Psalm—Psalm 23. I learned this through meditation exercises, and have made it my own. It brings me to a place of joy and peace and is a taste of Heaven.

A PSALM OF DAVID

The Lord is my shepherd;
I shall not want.
He makes me to lie down in green pastures;
He leads me beside the still waters.
He restores my soul;
He leads me in the paths of righteousness
For His name's sake.
Yea, though I walk through the valley of the shadow of death,
I will fear no evil;
For You are with me;
Your rod and Your staff, they comfort me.
You prepare a table before me in the presence of my enemies;
You anoint my head with oil;
My cup runs over.
Surely goodness and mercy shall follow me
All the days of my life;
And I will dwell in the house of the Lord forever. (NKJV)

Here's my interpretation of Psalm 23. It's a beautiful picture. Acknowledge that Jesus is your Shepherd, and He will lead you to the place of rest and peace, the green meadows. He will lead you to the still waters of refreshment and revive you and heal your soul. If you follow Him, He will lead you down the right paths of life, because you belong to Him, and He loves you. As you walk through those dark valleys and trials of life where you think you may not make it, you will fear no evil, because He is there with you, leading you through those crooked areas, guiding you in the right direction with His shepherd's staff. He will protect you from being lured from the rest of the flock. The feast He prepares is a celebration of victory you will have over your enemies. He invites you into His presence until you are filled up and victory is yours over the pride of life, the lust of the eyes, and the lust of the flesh. When He anoints your head with oil, you can do what must be done. The grace and empowerment of the Almighty God is yours, and you shall have the abundant life that Jesus Christ died on the cross for you to have—an overflowing life lived with God to the fullest, where goodness and mercy surround you and flow out of you to everyone in your world. This is walking in eternal life on earth, in peace, in the presence of God, every day and everywhere. From this place it is just a short step over to your eternal home in Heaven, where you will live with the Lord forever in the house He has prepared for you.